GW01458902

THE BEAN COOKBOOK

Windward

Windward is an imprint owned by W. H. Smith & Son Ltd. Registered No 237811 England, trading as:

WHS Distributors
St John's House
East Street
Leicester LE1 6NE

ISBN 0 7112 00882

This title was originated and published by Summit Books 176 South Creek Road, Dee Why West, N.S.W., Australia.

Frontispiece – From top – Chick Pea Dip, page 36; Dried Bean Patties, page 35, with Tahini Cream Sauce, page 108, and other traditional accompaniments.

Facing Half Title page – Boston Baked Beans, page 46, and Chili Con Carne, page 44.

THE BEAN COOKBOOK

Tess Mallos

WINDWARD

ACKNOWLEDGEMENTS

Writing a cookbook is a time-consuming process. Recipe testing and writing is only a small part of it. Playing sleuth in tracking down recipes, research, and gaining insight into the topic as a whole takes more time than you would believe, and the time of friends, acquaintances and contacts. It is these people I wish to acknowledge here.

Master Foods of Australia Pty. Ltd. for their helpful advice and assistance, particularly in regard to canned beans.

Tony Mayo of Riviana (Australia) Pty. Ltd., who patiently answered many queries on pulses imported by his company.

Stirling Macoboy, prolific author of garden books for answering questions relating to the botanical, and giving me many other gems of information.

Garth and Margaret Mathieson, owners of the El Terror Mexican Restaurant in Mosman, Sydney, for information on Mexican bean cooking.

Charmaine Solomon for her assistance with Indian and Sri Lankan information and recipes. May I recommend her book, *Indian Cooking for Pleasure*, if you want more Indian pulse recipes. We are both with the same publishing house.

Rosa Rodriguez, a charming Spanish friend, for her information on Spanish bean cooking.

June Hazel of The Bay Tree, Woollahra, Sydney, for lending me many of the props required for photography.

Last and not least I want to acknowledge the patience and fortitude of my husband John, and our children George, Anthony and Sue – their patience in putting up with the confusion of working at home, and their fortitude in consuming much of what is presented in these pages.

To my daughter Sue, who might need this book in the future more than she realises at this time.

CONTENTS

THE BEAN AND I

My earliest recollections of beans centre around my mother's fassoulatha, a fragrant Greek bean soup gently flavoured with olive oil and various vegetables. Black-eyed peas were usually used, and I still prefer these in this wholesome dish. So that mother would be sure we had a completely nourishing meal, keftethes (Greek meat patties) always accompanied it, and I remember liking the flavour combinations. Of course back in Greece, fassoulatha was (and still is) considered a meal in itself, with crusty bread and a hearty salad laced with chunks of pungent feta cheese. But meat was not plentiful in Greece then, while it certainly was here.

During my past twenty years' involvement in the food industry I have seen Australia's taste buds develop at an alarming rate. When working on promotional recipes early on, I was loath to go further than good basic Anglo-Saxon tucker with a fancy twist to it, with perhaps a curry or two (and very tame versions at that!). There almost always had to be meat, the more the better, and preferably the prime cuts. As our multi-cultural population of the post-war years introduced foods from their countries of origin, Australian tastes changed gradually, accepting more and more the vast variety of 'foreign' foods and learning to do more with the wide range of foods available locally.

Here, as elsewhere in the western world, a growing awareness of nutrition brought forth stores specializing in health foods, natural foods, organic foods, call them what you will (to me *all* foods are healthy, meat, eggs and butter included, providing the diet is balanced and excesses avoided).

These stores began stocking foods long available at Greek, Middle East, Asian and Armenian food stores, and thus began the latest development in the Australian cuisine, today as varied a cuisine as you would find anywhere in the world.

The last year or two has seen an increase, both here and abroad, in meat prices. In some countries these rises have been astronomical as nations which were not previously large meat eaters, began to want more and looked to meat producing nations to supply it. In turn the meat producing nations looked more closely at the cooking of their customers to find out how they had previously managed with little meat!

The food which came up time and time again was one almost as old as man himself, the pulse, the seed of leguminous plants – in short, the humble bean.

My aim in this book is to show the traditional meat-eater (meat in the broad sense), that food bills can be considerably reduced and hungry mouths filled by using pulses with meats, as accompaniments to meats, or as the occasional meat substitute. The majority of my recipes come from those countries which have had to rely on the pulse as a means of sustenance for countless generations, either for purely economical reasons, or because of religious taboos on certain foods.

And perhaps I should add that I am not going to convert the converted – if you follow a vegetarian diet, fine by me so long as you know that *only* the soya bean is as complete in proteins as meat, fish, chicken, eggs and cheese; that any other pulse can be complemented with grains and cereals; and, to be on the safe side, have eggs, milk and cheese daily.

Beans belong to the botanical family *Leguminosae,* the third largest plant family in the world with more than 12 000 members. After the grasses, which botanically encompass cereals and grains, beans are second in importance as a food source to man.

Vegetable foods rarely leave archaeological evidence, so it is difficult to date the time when beans were first used as a food.

What is known, though, is:

Beans and peas found near the Burmese border of Thailand have been carbon-dated at approximately 9750 BC.

In Peru evidence revealed beans were grown about 5680 BC.

The importance of the bean to Man is amply illustrated in two widely used expressions – 'full of beans' and 'I haven't a bean'.

Why use the bean to illustrate the point being made ? The answer is obvious.

Tess Mallos.

SPILLING THE BEANS ON BEAN NUTRITION

Vast quantities of canned baked beans are consumed annually in English-speaking countries. Surprisingly it is a highly nutritious, convenient meal, so continue to have your baked beans on toast knowing that a good proportion of your nutritional requirements is being provided.

All beans, peas and lentils are valuable in as much as they contribute vegetable protein, fibre, essential minerals and most of the vitamins. While the protein in beans (except for soya) is incomplete – that is not containing the full spectrum of amino acids which constitute complete protein – it can be complemented with proteins from nuts, grains and cereals.

Alternatively beans can combine with complete protein foods from the 'meat' group (meat, fish, poultry, eggs and cheese) to extend these foods and at the same time ensure adequate protein intake.

In recent years medical science has presented an excellent case for the increased consumption of dietary fibre as a preventive measure against heart disease. Ideally this should come from pulses (dried beans, peas and lentils), fruit and leafy vegetables. The advantage of a higher consumption of pulses lies in their ability to provide more of the essential nutrients required in the daily diet.

Beans lack few nutrients, the essential ones being vitamin B12 and C; the inclusion of foods from animal sources takes care of the B12, and the vitamin C can be provided through citrus fruits, tomatoes, fresh green peppers and, of course, bean sprouts.

Other essential nutrients contained in pulses are calcium, iron, thiamine, niacin, riboflavin, small amounts of vitamins E and K, and trace mineral elements.

Do not regard pulses as a vegetable. While the calorie count is higher than most vegetables, pulses are higher in other essential nutrients and should be used as an extender or replacement for meat, poultry, fish etc. For those who count calories, one cup of plainly cooked beans averages at about 180 calories.

BASIC BEAN COOKING

While it is common practice to soak beans overnight, I do not advocate it unless absolutely necessary. If you have ever wondered why beans disagree with you, the problem undoubtedly lies in the overnight soaking.

Beans can ferment even over a few hours, and though the water might be changed before cooking, the damage has been done. Where long soaking is required or preferred, place soaking beans in a cool place such as a cool larder, or even in the refrigerator, otherwise follow the quick-soak method.

Because beans contain certain vitamins that are water soluble, in most cases I recommend thorough washing before soaking, and using the soaking water for cooking. After all, if beans are to play an important role in general nutrition, as many nutrients as possible must be retained. Basic soaking details are given here, with further recommendations given under the individual beans detailed in Finger on the Pulse.

Basic Bean Preparation: Pick over beans to remove small stones and any beans that are discoloured. This is more easily done by spreading them out on a tray. Put beans into a bowl and fill with cold water, stir well and remove any that float. Now wash well in several changes of cold water and drain.

Slow Soaking: Only certain beans will require long soaking. Put washed beans in a bowl, add amount of water specified in recipe (generally in the proportion of 3 parts water to one of beans). Cover bowl and put in a cool place (larder or refrigerator). Use soaking water for cooking, unless otherwise specified.

Slow Salt Soak: This method is an alternative to a plain water soak in that the salt used minimises the risk of beans fermenting. Add 2 teaspoons salt to each 2 cups (1lb) beans and water. They can be left at room temperature but the water must be drained off and fresh water added before cooking.

Quick Soaking: Put washed beans and amount of water specified into a pan and bring to the boil, uncovered. Boil 2 minutes, cover pan and remove from heat. Leave aside for 1-2 hours until beans are plump.

Basic Bean Cooking: Place beans and soaking liquid in a heavy pan, or leave in pan in which they have been quick-soaked. Bring to the boil, cover and boil gently for time specified under individual bean varieties. Add salt towards end of cooking, as adding it too soon lengthens cooking time considerably. Likewise, large quantities of acid ingredients such as tomatoes and wine should not be added too soon, though small amounts can be added early in cooking. Be guided by recipe instructions.

Basic Lentil and Split Pea Cooking: Pick over lentils or split peas to remove any damaged ones and small stones. Put into a bowl and cover with water, stir and remove any that float. Rinse in several changes of water then proceed with recipe. It is not necessary to pre-soak, unless the pulse is to be used in the raw state. Where this is required, details are given in recipes.

An important cooking tip with such pulses is not to stir once gentle boiling begins. This is a Greek cooking tip passed on to me by my mother, as she claimed stirring caused the split peas or lentils to catch on the base of the pan. I have always followed this method and only ever had problems when I have absent-mindedly stirred the pan contents.

Microwave Oven Soaking and Cooking: Not a time saver at all. It takes just as long by conventional means as microwave cooking manuals recommend that beans be cooked at the 'defrost' setting, a very low microwave frequency. In fact lentils and split peas take longer to cook than by conventional means. Of course cooked bean and lentil dishes reheat very well in the microwave oven.

Pressure Cooking: For quick cooking a pressure cooker is heartily recommended. Where beans are cooked with many flavouring ingredients, long, slow cooking is preferable so that the beans absorb the flavours. However many recipes require plain cooked beans to begin with, and a pressure cooker is a definite time saver here. As a general guide suitable recipes are those where a minimum of flavourings are added early in cooking. The soaked beans and liquid must only fill the cooker by one-third. A 5.5 litre (9½ imperial pint or 12 US pint) pressure cooker will take up to 2½ cups (1lb) beans.

1. Pre-soak the beans using either slow or quick-soak methods.
2. Put beans and soaking water into cooker, adding any flavouring ingredients if necessary at beginning of cooking (no salt or acid ingredients, though a small amount of bacon bones or scalded salt pork may be added).
3. Bring open cooker to the boil on high heat, skimming well if necessary. Reduce heat so that contents are boiling gently without rising in the cooker.
4. Put on lid fitted with weight required for high pressure (the heaviest weight) and keep cooker on the same heat until pressure is reached. Time from this point, following given times for the various beans. Reduce pressure as instructed in your cooker's manual.

Cooking Times

Adzuki: **20 minutes**
Black (Mexican): **15 minutes**
Black-eyed: **10 minutes**
Borlotti (Roman): **15 minutes**
Broad: **20 minutes**
Butter: **20 minutes**
Cannellini (white kidney): **15 minutes**
Chick peas (garbanzo): **20 minutes**
Dutch brown: **20 minutes**
Ful (Egyptian brown): **30 minutes**
Haricot (navy): **15 minutes**
Lima (large): **15 minutes**
Lima (small): **10 minutes**
Pink: **15 minutes**
Pinto: **20 minutes**
Red Kidney: **15 minutes**
Saluggia: **15 minutes**
Soya: **30 minutes**

CANNED BEANS

For quick-to-prepare meals, canned beans are a boon to the busy cook. While all bean varieties are not available in cans, there is a good can range of the most popular beans. As they are already cooked in the can, preparation and cooking of bean dishes is reduced to a minimum with obvious savings in fuel costs. Follow this guide to substitute canned beans for the dried beans used in recipes.

1 cup dried beans — use 2 300 g (10 oz) cans or 1 675 g (1 lb) can.
1½ cups dried beans — use 2 440 g (1 lb) cans.

Minestrone Genoese, page 22, with Pesto Sauce, page 99.

1. Butter beans.
2. Red kidney beans.
3. Chick peas or garbanzo beans.
4. Borlotti or cranberry beans – three varieties are shown to illustrate differences in shadings and markings. Also known as Roman beans.
5. Lima beans – large white, small green and small white.
6. Egyptian brown beans (ful).
7. Haricot, navy or pea beans.
8. Pinto beans.
9. Black-eyed beans or peas, also known as cowpeas.
10. Brown beans, also known as Dutch or African brown beans.
11. Brown and green lentils, also known as continental lentils.
12. Split red lentils.
13. Mung beans or green gram.
14. Black beans – Chinese.
15. Adzuki beans.
16. Soya beans.
17. Broad beans.
18. Great Northern beans, often sold as cannellini beans.
19. Black beans – Mexican. Also known as turtle beans.
20. Pink beans.
21. Lupins.
22. Saluggia beans – often sold as cranberry beans.
23. Yellow split peas.
24. Green split peas.

FINGER ON THE PULSE

Bean and lentil cooking times can vary considerably. It is generally believed that pulses from new season's crops take less cooking time than those which have been stored for a long period. This might be true of some pulses but the other factors which influence cooking times are where the beans were grown and the type of soil and prevailing climatic conditions.

For example soya beans can be notoriously stubborn, and while I have cooked them in 3½-4 hours, some batches have taken almost twice as long as soya beans are grown locally and imported. Such a difference is the exception rather then the rule – you will find that generally the time might only need to be extended for ½-1 hour.

I advise the careful monitoring of the beans when you want to end up with tender beans still holding their shape; if they are to be puréed, mashed or otherwise processed, it doesn't matter much if they break up during cooking. Therefore use time given as a guide only. If you keep large stocks of particular beans, make a note of the actual cooking time for future reference.

ADZUKI BEANS: tiny reddish brown beans popular in Asian cooking, particularly Chinese and Japanese. In both these cuisines the beans are mainly used for sweet dishes. One Japanese savoury dish reserved for special celebrations is Sekihan – cooked beans mashed to a paste and spread on top of bowls of steamed glutinous rice.

The beans are also used for sprouting, and made into sweetened red bean paste (dow saah) – while this is readily available canned, it is easily made in your kitchen (page 114). Wash beans and soak in cold water for 2-3 hours, then boil gently for 1½-2 hours.

BLACK BEANS (CHINESE): small, almost round, black beans which are green under the skin. In China and Thailand they are regarded as having medicinal properties, particularly for pregnant women, as it is claimed they thicken the blood and strengthen the system. Otherwise the beans are not used a great deal in cooking. The tiny salted black beans prepared in China and Taiwan use another even smaller black bean not available in dried form outside the area.

The salted, fermented beans are available in bulk or canned in brine. Those purchased loose should be soaked in warm water for 10 minutes, drained and rinsed before use. Canned salted black beans only require a quick rinse under cold water.

BLACK BEANS (MEXICAN): shiny, black kidney-shaped beans much used in Mexican and Caribbean cooking. The size can vary according to the area in which they are grown and the prevailing conditions. When good crops allow, the beans are exported to the United Kingdom, but are difficult, if impossible, to find in Australia. A popular bean in the United States, particularly in the Southern and West Coast regions where Mexican cooking is favoured.

Very flavourful, smooth-textured beans, they can be slow or quick soaked and require about 2 hours gentle boiling. Avocado leaf, toasted and crumbled, adds an interesting flavour and is regarded as a means of eliminating the discomfort beans can cause. For the same reason fresh coriander and dried oregano are used in Mexican bean cooking.

BLACK-EYED BEANS: sometimes called black-eyed peas, they are a small kidney-shaped bean, creamy-white in colour with a black spot on the skin resembling an eye. They have a very pleasant, slightly sweet flavour. It is often preferable to pour off the soaking water and add fresh water for cooking. This prevents the discolouration of the finished dish, as the black spot leaches into the cooking liquid. I don't mind the colour change, much preferring it to the loss of nutrients. Quick soaking is recommended, and the beans cook quickly – in about 1 hour. Used widely in Greek, Middle Eastern and Indian cooking, and very popular in the United States.

BLACK GRAM: tiny black pulse similar in size and shape to the mung bean, and used in Indian cooking. When purchased they are likely to look more grey than black, because of fine dust. More often black gram are available skinned and split, creamy in colour.

The husked black gram is used with rice for Dhosai, a popular South Indian pancake, or for making Dhal (spiced lentil purée). Known in India (and Indian food stores) as urad when whole and urad dhal when husked and split.

BORLOTTI: known as Roman or cranberry beans in the U.S. Large kidney-shaped beans, plump and colourful. Can be beige in colour, attractively speckled with claret-coloured markings; sometimes they are a more definite brown with the same markings or an even deeper background colour with the speckles almost covering the bean. The latter are usually called either borlotti or cranberry, depending on the whim of the packager or storekeeper. Point is they are all varieties of the same bean, the colour differences depending on the country of origin.

A popular bean in Italian cooking (and to a lesser extent in the Middle East), with a smooth texture and excellent ham-like flavour readily absorbing other flavours. May be used in place of pinto or red kidney beans. Slow or quick soak and boil for about 1½ hours or longer depending on where they were grown.

BROAD BEANS: range in colour from olive green to brown. Sometimes all green beans are available, but usually they vary in colour from green through deep cream to brown. Green beans signify a new season's crop and take less time to cook. Slow or quick soak, change water and cook for about 2½ hours, though the flavour is disappointing when compared with fresh broad beans.

Popular in the Mediterranean and Middle East, Egypt and Italy in particular. When prepared in these regions, the beans are slow soaked for 48 hours with frequent changes of water so that the rather leathery skin may be removed before cooking. Used in purées, soups and bean patties.

Soaked, uncooked beans are used for bean patties such as Tameya and Falafel – if cooked beans are used, the patties disintegrate when fried. Husked broad beans are sometimes available and save a lot of preparation time; they are cream in colour and only require 8-12 hours soaking and 1½ hours cooking.

BROWN BEANS: also known as Dutch or African brown beans, they are small to medium-sized, shiny, brown kidney-shaped beans. Country of origin can determine size and length of cooking time. I have found the smaller beans take longer to cook than the larger ones. Similar in flavour and texture to red kidney beans, they may be used as a substitute for these beans. The Dutch like these mixed with fried onions and smoked speck or fatty bacon. Also a good bean for mixed bean soups or combined with other beans for salads. Slow or quick soak and boil gently for 1½-2½ hours.

BUTTER BEANS: very large, plump white beans grown in Madagascar. Very popular in England, favoured for their buttery flavour and floury texture, and often served puréed with cream added as an accompaniment to roast pork. They also go well in bean salads when slow soaking is preferred so that the beans stay intact. They have a very fine skin and the quick soaking tends to lift it off prematurely. When using as a purée, quick soaking is in order. Boil gently for 2 hours. Large white lima beans may be substituted.

CANNELLINI: white kidney beans, larger than the haricot and squared off at the ends. True cannellini beans are native to South America, the only source of these beans. As supplies are intermittent, Great Northern beans from the United States are generally sold as cannellini beans in Europe and other Western nations. Use in any recipe calling for haricot (navy) or white kidney beans. Slow or quick soak and boil gently for 1½ hours.

CHICK PEAS OR GARBANZO BEANS: rounded in shape, rough textured with a chicken beak-shaped peak at one end, hence their name. Creamy fawn in colour. They have a nutty, earthy flavour and are much favoured in Spanish, Italian, Greek, Armenian, Middle Eastern and Indian cooking. While these are generally slow soaked, I find quick soaking is just as effective. Slow soaking is necessary when the pulse is used for Falafel as raw softened peas are required. If cooked peas are used, the Falafel disintegrate when fried; quick soaking tends to cook the peas a little.

Purists in Greek and Armenian cooking prefer to remove the skins after soaking. Rub handfuls of peas together or spread on a tray and roll a rolling pin over them, exerting pressure. Float off skins and repeat until all are skinned. Sometimes chick peas are available ready-skinned, when they resemble split peas, though they are creamy in colour and slightly larger. Armenian and Asian food stores are supply sources. Whole soaked peas cook in 2½ hours, the skinned peas in 1½ hours. Ideal for pressure cooking.

CRANBERRY: see *Borlotti.*

EGYPTIAN BROWN BEANS (FUL): a member of the broad bean family, these small rounded beans range in colour from fawn to deep purple-brown. They have been a staple food in Egypt from ancient times, and are just as popular today. Used mainly for Ful Medamis, which is traditionally cooked very slowly for 6 hours or more. Pressure cooking gives the same results in a fraction of the time. For normal cooking, slow or quick soak and boil gently for 2½-3 hours.

FLAGEOLET: a member of the haricot bean family, these small, slender beans reminded someone of a flute, hence their name. Shelled when mature but still green, their colour remains after drying. Favoured in French cooking as a vegetable accompaniment, particularly with roast leg of lamb. A more expensive bean, you are likely to find them in gourmet food stores; more often than not they are only available canned. If you ever come across the dried beans, quick soak and boil gently for 1-1½ hours. Add an onion and bay leaf to the beans during cooking for a typically French flavour.

GARBANZO BEANS: see *Chick Peas.*

GREAT NORTHERN: medium-sized white kidney beans grown in the United States. They are similar to cannellini beans, being a little smaller and rounded at each end. The cannellini beans you buy are more likely to be Great Northern. May be used in any recipe specifying cannellini or haricot (navy) beans. Quick soak and boil gently for 1½ hours.

HARICOT (NAVY): small white beans oval in shape. One of the most widely used, they are the beans canned with various flavoured tomato sauces to become the perennial favourite, Baked Beans. Quick soaking is preferred, then boil gently for 1½ hours. Other small white beans such as cannellini and Great Northern may be substituted in recipes.

LENTILS: two varieties of lentils are widely available – split red lentils, and brown or green lentils (continental lentils), a flattish round pulse with skin intact. When the lens was developed it was so named because of its resemblance to the double-convexed shape of the lentil.

These pulses have sustained man for countless centuries and in some areas are as important in today's diet as they were from earliest times. Indian cooking is renowned for its lentil-based dishes. (See *black gram* and *mung beans*). No need to pre-soak. Split red lentils cook in 30 minutes; continental lentils take 1-1½ hours. Continental lentils are also good for sprouting (see page 109).

LIMA: one of the most popular beans, limas can be small green or white (baby limas) or the larger white bean. Kidney-shaped and flat, they have a pleasant, sweetish flavour and floury texture. Slow or quick soak, then boil gently for 1-1½ hours, depending on size. A popular canned bean, the lima is good in both hot dishes and salads. The large beans may be used as a substitute for butter beans in recipes.

LUPINS: this edible pulse in its natural form has long been used as a snack food in Italy and parts of the Middle East, though the plant itself is used as cattle fodder elsewhere. Lupins are high in alkaloids and must be specially prepared to rid them of their bitterness. (See recipe for Lupini, page 39).

MUNG BEANS: also known as green beans and green gram. They are tiny beans with a moss green skin and most widely used for sprouting. Used whole in the cooking of Afghanistan and Sri Lanka. When husked and split, they become the mung dhal of Indian cooking. Also ground to a flour for Asian sweets. When cooking either the whole or husked bean, there is no need to pre-soak. Boil gently for 45 minutes to 1 hour.

PEANUTS: the peanut, or groundnut as it is known in Africa, is a strange member of the leguminous plant family, but a member nonetheless and an important one. The flower spikes bend to the ground and the pods form and ripen under the ground. Peanuts are second to soya beans in nutritional value, and because of their easy preparation and flavour, add an interesting and varied dimension to bean cooking.

PEAS, WHOLE DRIED: also called blue peas, they are a poor substitute for fresh peas, their only advantage being in easy storage and low cost. As they usually cook to a mush no matter how careful you are, it is far better to use green split peas. Their only advantage over the split peas is that you add valuable fibre to the diet. If you must cook them, soak overnight with a pinch of bicarbonate of soda and 1 teaspoon salt to 1 cup peas. Drain, add fresh water and boil for about 1 hour, adding salt and a little sugar towards end of cooking.

PINK BEANS: dusky pink kidney beans of medium size, popular in Mexican cooking. Available in North America, but difficult to find outside the American continent. Red kidney or pinto beans may be used in place of pink beans in recipes. Slow or quick soak and boil gently for 1½-2 hours.

PINTO BEANS: attractive beige coloured beans speckled with brown, pintos have always been a staple food of the Mexicans. In recent years pintos have become more readily available outside the Americas. When cooked they become a pleasant dusky pink with an appetizingly savoury flavour and smooth texture. Slow or quick soak and boil gently for 2-2½ hours. As Mexican bean recipes often call for mashed or puréed beans, they are suitable for pressure cooking. Borlotti beans are a good substitute.

RED KIDNEY: one of the most widely used beans, bright red in colour with the characteristic kidney shape. Size and depth of colour varies according to where they were grown. Their best known use is for Chili Con Carne (page 44), but their pleasant flavour and smooth texture makes them ideal for soups, substantial bean dishes and salads. One of the most popular beans for canning, and as they are so versatile, it is worthwhile having a few cans on hand for quick meal preparation.

Slow or quick soak beans, and boil gently for 1–1½ hours. Red kidney beans may be used in place of borlotti (Roman), pink and pinto beans in recipes.

SALUGGIA: while somewhat similar in appearance and flavour to borlotti beans, saluggia are smaller, slightly darker and with the speckled markings almost covering some of the beans, while hardly noticeable on others. A quick look at them has you wondering if your supplier has thrown in some red kidney and brown beans. Saluggia are often marketed as cranberry beans. Slow or quick soak and boil gently for 1½ hours.

SOYA BEANS: small oval shaped beans, very hard and buff-coloured. The most nutritious of all the beans as they contain the full spectrum of amino acids which constitutes complete protein. Also high in fat content, they are regarded as a perfect meat substitute and ideal for vegetarian cooking. As they require long cooking to make them tender and are uninspiring in flavour, there are other more interesting beans to choose from when beans are to be enjoyed for their own sake.

Slow or quick soak, drain, rinse and add fresh water for cooking as soya beans are high in yeast content, the factor which is likely to cause digestive problems. Boil gently for 3½-4 hours, beginning with a greater proportion of water to beans than normally required. Check during cooking to ensure there is sufficient liquid. Use in place of haricot, cannellini, Great Northern or red kidney beans, increasing cooking times. The by-products of soya beans are a more attractive culinary proposition (see *Offshoots*, page 18).

SPLIT PEAS: both green and yellow split peas are readily available. Most widely used for thick, warming pea soups. Yellow split peas may be used in place of lentils in many recipes, particularly Indian dishes. Do not pre-soak. Boil gently for 1-1½ hours without stirring otherwise they tend to stick to the base of the pan.

TWO INTERESTING RELATIVES

As it is the pods rather than the seeds that are used, I have dealt with the following two members of the *Leguminosae* family separately.

CAROB OR ST. JOHN'S BREAD: the mature bean pod has been a popular snack food in the Middle East for countless centuries. It is said that John the Baptist, in his wanderings in the wilderness, ate the carob bean pod for survival, hence the alternative name. The pod is also processed to make a molasses called dibs. Combined with tahini (sesame seed paste) it is spread on flat bread and eaten for breakfast or as a snack.

With the trend to health or natural foods, the carob in recent years has been acclaimed in the Western world as a chocolate substitute as it does not contain the fats, caffeine and other properties which have made cocoa and chocolate undesirable to many.

From the chocolate flavoured pod, two basic products are made which can be used very successfully as cocoa and chocolate substitutes. Carob powder may be used in similar ways to cocoa powder, though additions such as vanilla and decaffeinated coffee make it more acceptable in flavour.

Block carob is made in combination with lecithin, raw sugar, soya protein, milk powder *etcetera* and can be dark, light, or combined with nuts or dried fruit for a very successful chocolate bar substitute. The dark block carob is the one I recommend for cooking purposes. Health food stores are well stocked with these lines.

TAMARIND: the word Tamarind comes from the Arabic, and literally means 'date of India'. The large fleshy pod of this tropical tree is strongly acid and is favoured for this quality. Tamarind is used in the cooking of India, Pakistan and Middle East countries. A refreshing beverage is also made and relished in these regions.

Tamarind pods are available in Asian and health food stores, usually pressed together in a firm, somewhat sticky mass. To use in cooking, put specified amount in hot water, breaking it up with fingertips. Leave to soak for 10-15 minutes and pass through a fine sieve set over a bowl, rubbing with the back of a spoon to separate pulp from fibres and seeds. Discard fibres and seeds and use liquid. Instant tamarind paste is also available and only requires to be blended with hot water. Use 1 teaspoon instant tamarind paste in place of 1 tablespoon tamarind pulp. Lemon juice may be used as a substitute in recipes, with the juice of 1 medium-sized lemon equivalent in sourness to 1 tablespoon tamarind pulp dissolved in ¼ cup hot water.

OFFSHOOTS

As I am basically exploring the pulse cooking of countries which have relied heavily on vegetable proteins for nutrition, this book would not be complete without detailing the numerous by-products of the pulse, or offshoots as I choose to call them.

In China, Japan and other Asian countries, these offshoots are more important than the actual beans. In regions of China and Japan their quick methods of cooking evolved more because of lack of fuel than any other reason, and beans in their dry state take a lot of cooking. Hence the importance of bean curd, bean shoots, soya sauce, fermented beans, bean pastes and so on.

The strict vegetarians of India make wide use of flours ground from pulses to add variety to their cooking, giving another dimension to pulse cooking.

As Chinese, Japanese and Indian cooking can be complicated I have only given a few recipes using some of these products.

BEAN CURD – Dow foo (Chinese): A bland, soft curd compressed into cakes. Creamy white in colour with the consistency of a very firm custard. Itself bland in flavour, bean curd absorbs other flavours readily. As it is very rich in complete proteins, it is a valuable addition to the Asian diet. It is obtainable from Chinese and Japanese food stores usually in 5cm (2 inch) squares. Store in water in a sealed container in refrigerator, changing water daily. Keeps 1 week or more. Discard if it becomes spotted with red mould. Directions for making bean curd are given in recipe section – see page 107.

BEAN CURD – Tofu (Japanese): Similar to Dow foo, but a little sweeter in flavour and more delicate in texture. Also available packaged in powdered form at Japanese food stores and easily made at home.

YELLOW BEAN CURD – Taukwa (Chinese): bean curd compressed for longer period so that it is firmer in texture. Sometimes dyed artificially with a yellow dye and available at Chinese food stores. It is principally used for stuffing and deep frying. To make a reasonable substitute at home, place soft bean curd squares on a tea-towel in a flat dish, spacing them well apart. Top with another towel and put a flat dish or board on top of the curd. Weigh down evenly with weights (a heavy book or two will do — about 1kg or 2lbs in weight) and leave until compressed to half original thickness.

COMPRESSED BEAN CURD — Taufu kan (Chinese): bean curd compressed until it is a quarter of original thickness — see directions under *Yellow Bean Curd.* Good shredded and mixed into other vegetables as a salad.

DRIED BEAN CURD (sheets and twists). The sheets (taufu juk) are made from bean curd compressed until flat and allowed to dry. Usually wiped with a damp cloth to clean and soften them. The twists (taufu kee) are made from the skin formed when making bean curd. (See *Bean Curd* recipe, page 107). These can be fried in hot oil until puffed and added to vegetable dishes just before serving, or cut into short lengths, soaked in hot water for 15 minutes and used in the same way.

FERMENTED RED BEAN CURD and **BEAN CURD CHEESE:** sold in tins or jars, it can be reddish brown or creamy. Salty and highly savoury, amounts should be adjusted to suit taste, as these are used as a seasoning rather than a food. Though usually served with bland foods, these curds add a delightful savoury taste to meat and vegetable dishes.

BEAN SPROUTS: mung beans, adzuki beans or brown lentils (those with skin on) can be used for sprouting. The idea is to use small, low cost beans — it is uneconomical to use soya or other larger beans, unless you like to experiment with flavours and textures. Bean sprouts are high in vitamins A and C, and should be eaten raw or very lightly cooked. For more detail see recipe for making your own bean sprouts, page 109.

SOYA SAUCE: this universally known condiment is made from salted and fermented soya beans. While soya sauce is essential for Asian cooking, it is making more frequent appearances in Western recipes because of its salty, savoury flavour, dark colour and low calorie content.

CHICK PEA FLOUR: also known as besan or channa dhal flour and available at Asian food stores. Check details on package carefully as lentil flour is sometimes labelled as besan. Used in Indian cooking for batters and special occasion sweets, and, would you believe, in a Nice speciality called Socca (page 32).

LENTIL FLOUR: often labelled as besan, though a good supplier will have it more correctly labelled. Lentil flour can be made from ground lentils or split peas (these are called lentils or dhal in India, anyway). Generally used in a batter for coating vegetables as a substitute for chick pea flour. Any other recipe calling for chick pea flour must use this ingredient as the flavour is different to the lentil flour. Be guided by recipe instructions.

SOUPS

There is nothing timid about a bean soup – it is not a light, frivolous start to a meal, designed to titillate the palate and prepare the diner for more satisfying fare. With rare exceptions, bean and lentil soups are robust and nourishing, a good start to a meal if the following course is light, or a meal in itself when served with crusty fresh bread and a glass of wine.

Spanish Tripe and Chick Pea Soup

CALLOS

Serves: 6

1 cup (8 oz) chick peas
8 cups (4 imperial pints) water
2 pig's trotters, split and cut in pieces
750 g (1½ lb) tripe
3 smoked chorizo sausages
salt
freshly ground black pepper
¼ cup (2 fl oz) olive oil
2 cloves garlic, finely chopped
3 teaspoons paprika
¼ teaspoon chili powder
¼ cup (1 oz) plain flour

Wash chick peas well, put in deep pan with 3 cups water and bring to the boil. Boil 2 minutes, cover and remove from heat. Leave for 1 hour or until plump. Add remaining water to pot with rinsed pig's trotters and bring to the boil, skimming when required. Cover and simmer gently for 1½ hours. Wash tripe well and cut into 2 cm (¾ inch) squares. Add to pan, cover and cook for further hour or until chick peas are tender. Remove trotters, trim off meat and return meat to soup.

Cut sausages into 1 cm (½ inch) slices and add to soup with salt and pepper to taste. Cover and simmer for 30 minutes.

Place a frying pan on medium heat and add olive oil and garlic. When garlic is golden brown stir in paprika, chili powder and flour. Cook for 1 minute then pour into soup, stirring constantly. Let soup bubble gently for 2 minutes.

Serve in deep plates with crusty bread.

Lentil and Tamarind Soup

RASAM

Serves: 6

Popularly known as Pepperwater, Rasam can be a thin or slightly thickened liquid. Many recipes exist for this sour-hot soup, ranging from those with no lentils at all to those lightly thickened with lentils. Versions in between use the water from cooked lentils for added nutrition and flavour. I have selected one thickened with lentils as it can be used as a light soup, as a spicy, light sauce to add flavour and moistness to dry Indian dishes, or sipped at the end of a meal to aid digestion. While a lentil known as toor dhal is traditionally used (split and husked pigeon peas), yellow split peas work just as well, though maybe not for an Indian.

½ cup (4 oz) yellow split peas
5 cups (2½ imperial pints) water
1 medium-sized ripe tomato, peeled and diced
1 tablespoon tamarind pulp (see page 18)
2 cloves garlic, crushed
½ teaspoon ground cummin
1 teaspoon freshly ground black pepper
¼ teaspoon ground turmeric
salt to taste
1 tablespoon oil
1 teaspoon black mustard seeds
1 dried chili, halved and seeds removed

Pick over split peas and wash well. Put in a pan with 4 cups water and bring to the boil. Add tomato, cover and boil gently for 45 minutes-1 hour until peas are very soft and practically dissolved into the liquid. Meanwhile soak tamarind in remaining heated water for 10-15 minutes and strain pulp into soup. Add garlic, cummin, pepper and turmeric, and add salt to taste (about 2 teaspoons). Cover and simmer for further 30 minutes.

In a small pan heat oil and add mustard seeds and chili. When seeds pop and chili is brown pour into simmering soup. Stir and return to the boil. Serve hot in small bowls as a soup, or in a larger bowl to be added to other Indian foods according to individual taste.

Egyptian Broad Bean Soup

FUL NABED

Serves: 6

3 cups (1½ lbs) dried broad beans
cold water
1 teaspoon ground cummin
salt
freshly ground black pepper
¼ cup (2 fl oz) olive oil
1 tablespoon lemon juice
For serving:
finely chopped parsley
lemon wedges

Cover beans well with cold water and soak for 48 hours, changing water twice each day. Remove skins by pressing each bean firmly, tearing skin with fingernail if necessary. Put into pan with 6 cups water, bring to slow simmer, cover and simmer gently for 1½ hours until very soft. Press through a sieve or purée in a blender. Return to pan and add cummin, salt and pepper to taste, olive oil and lemon juice. Stir over gentle heat until bubbling. Serve hot in deep bowls garnished with chopped parsley. Lemon juice is squeezed on according to individual taste. Arab flat bread or other bread should accompany this soup.

Minestrone Genoese

Serves 8-10

In her regional cooking, Italy offers many versions of Minestrone. This one from Genoa is a good vegetarian soup. By adding diced fried bacon with the vegetables and using a good beef stock in place of the water, you can turn this version into the standard Minestrone. Serve with lots of grated Parmesan cheese instead of the Pesto Sauce, which is a Genoese speciality.

¾ cup (6 oz) cannellini or haricot (navy) beans
6 cups (3 imperial pints) water
¼ cup (2 fl oz) olive oil
2 cloves garlic, crushed
2 small onions, sliced
1 large carrot, diced
1 stalk celery, sliced
1 leek, washed well and chopped
1 white turnip, peeled and diced
500 g (1 lb) ripe tomatoes, peeled, seeded and chopped
2 tablespoons tomato paste
½ teaspoon sugar
salt
freshly ground black pepper
125 g (4 oz) green beans, sliced in short lengths
250 g (8 oz) green peas, shelled
250 g (8 oz) potatoes, peeled and diced
¼ white cabbage, coarsely shredded
2 tablespoons chopped parsley
½ cup (4 oz) risone noodles or broken thin spaghetti
Pesto Sauce (page 99)
grated Parmesan cheese, optional

Wash beans well, put in a large pan with half the water and bring to the boil. Boil 2 minutes, cover and remove from heat. Leave for 1 hour until beans are plump. Return to the boil and simmer, covered, for 1 hour or until beans are fairly tender. In a frying pan heat the oil, add onion and fry gently until transparent. Add garlic, cook a few seconds, then add carrot, celery, leek and turnip. Fry for 5 minutes and pour into beans. Add remaining water, tomatoes, tomato paste and sugar and add salt and pepper to taste. Cover and cook for 30 minutes. Add beans, peas and potatoes and cook for further 30 minutes.

Lastly stir in shredded cabbage, parsley and pasta and boil, uncovered, on medium heat until pasta is tender. Add more water if soup begins to catch on base of pan. Soup should be very thick. Serve in a tureen with separate bowls of Pesto Sauce and Parmesan cheese to be stirred into individual serves according to taste.

Green Pea Soup

Serves: 6-8

2 cups (1 lb) split green peas
1 large onion, chopped
1 carrot, quartered
500 g (1 lb) ham bone or 1 ham hock
6 cups (3 imperial pints) water
salt
freshly ground white pepper
croutons for serving

Pick over split peas and wash well. Place in a heavy pan with onion and carrot. Rinse ham bone or hock and add to pan with the water. Bring slowly to the boil, skimming when necessary. When simmering gently, reduce heat to low, cover and cook gently for 2 hours. Do not stir during cooking. When peas are very soft, remove carrot pieces and discard. Lift out ham bone or hock and trim off any meat. Chop finely and return to soup with salt and pepper to taste. Stir well to a purée, or for a finer texture, purée in batches in food processor or blender before adding the ham pieces. Serve in a tureen with croutons in a separate bowl.

DUTCH PEA SOUP

Follow above directions, using 2 pig's trotters, split and washed, instead of the ham bones or hock. When cooked remove trotters and discard. Purée soup, return to pan and season to taste. Meanwhile, in a separate pan gently heat a rookwurst sausage in simmering water. Slice the cooked sausage and add to the tureen of soup. Served with crusty brown bread and butter, Dutch Pea Soup is a meal in itself.

Mexican Bean Soup

Serves: 6-8

1 quantity Frijoles de Olla (page 43)
For serving:
shredded mature cheddar cheese or sour cream
finely chopped spring onions (scallions)

Prepare Frijoles de Olla as directed, using pinto or pink beans. Remove bacon bones but do not remove the cup of beans for mashing. When cooked, purée beans and liquid in a blender or food processor in three batches. Return to pan and reheat. Serve hot in deep plates with a dollop of sour cream in the centre and sprinkle with chopped spring onions. A good vegetarian soup if vegetable stock is used in place of bacon bones, and oil instead of lard.

Lentil and Silverbeet Soup

Serves: 5-6

1½ cups brown lentils
6 cups cold water
8-10 leaves silverbeet (Swiss chard)
1 large onion, finely chopped
3 cloves garlic, finely chopped
¼ cup olive oil
¼ cup chopped coriander leaves
salt
freshly ground black pepper
¼ cup lemon juice
lemon wedges for serving

Wash lentils well and place in a heavy pan with the cold water. Bring to the boil, skimming if necessary, then cover and simmer gently for 1 hour or until lentils are soft. Wash silverbeet well and cut off stems. (Stems may be used as a separate vegetable for later meals.) Slit leaves down the middle then shred coarsely. Heat oil in a separate pan, add onion and fry gently until transparent. Stir in garlic and cook for a few seconds longer. Add shredded silverbeet to pan and fry, stirring often, until leaves wilt. Pour onion and silverbeet mixture into lentils, add salt and pepper to taste and the lemon juice. Cover and simmer gently for further 15-20 minutes. Serve soup in deep plates with lemon wedges for squeezing into soup according to individual taste. Flat Arab bread or other crusty bread is a necessary accompaniment.

Greek Bean Soup

FASSOULATHA

Serves: 6-8

2 cups (1 lb) dried haricot (navy), cannellini, lima or black-eyed beans
8 cups (4 imperial pints) water
1 large onion, finely chopped
1½ cups chopped, peeled tomatoes
2 tablespoons tomato paste
1 cup chopped celery, including leaves
1 cup diced carrot
¼ cup chopped parsley
⅓ cup (3 fl oz) olive oil
freshly ground black pepper
½ teaspoon sugar
salt
For serving:
chopped parsley

Wash beans well in several changes of water. Place in a large pot with the 8 cups water and bring to the boil. Boil for 2 minutes, remove from heat and leave pan covered 1-2 hours until beans become plump. Add remaining ingredients except salt and bring to the boil. Cover pan and boil gently for 1½ hours. Add salt to taste and cook for further 30-60 minutes until beans are tender. Again time depends on beans. Serve hot in soup plates, sprinkling chopped parsley on each serve. Crusty bread, black olives, cheese and wine can accompany fassoulatha for a complete meal.

Bean Curd Prawn Sour Hot Soup

Serves: 6

2 cakes bean curd (about 125g or 4 oz)
4 Chinese dried mushrooms
1 cup (8 fl oz) warm water
60 g (2 oz) bamboo shoots
125 g (4 oz) uncooked shrimp or small prawns
6 spring onions (scallions)
2 tablespoons oil
4 cups (2 imperial pints) chicken stock
2 tablespoons soya sauce
2-3 tablespoons brown vinegar
salt
freshly ground black pepper
1½ tablespoons cornflour
1 egg
½ teaspoon sesame oil, optional
diagonally sliced spring onion tops for garnish

Rinse bean curd under cold, running water, drain carefully and cut into 1 cm (½ inch) cubes. Leave in colander to drain thoroughly. Soak mushrooms in the warm water for 15 minutes until spongy, drain, reserving water, remove stems and discard. Slice mushrooms into thin shreds. Cut bamboo shoot into shreds. Shell shrimp or prawns, devein if necessary, and rinse briefly. Slice spring onions diagonally, cutting as finely as possible and including some of green top. Put some sliced green tops aside for garnish.

Heat oil in a deep pan and stir-fry mushrooms and bamboo shoot for 2 minutes, add spring onion and fry for further minute. Add chicken stock and mushroom liquid and bring to the boil. Reduce heat so that soup simmers gently and add shrimp and diced bean curd. Cook gently until shrimp turn pink, but do not boil vigorously. Add soya sauce and vinegar, salt and pepper to taste. Blend cornflour with a little cold water and stir into simmering soup. When thickened let soup bubble very gently for 1 minute. Beat egg well and pour into soup, stirring constantly so that egg forms shreds. Add sesame oil if used and serve immediately, garnishing each serve with shredded spring onion tops.

Sour Lentil Soup

Serves: 6

2 cups (1 lb) brown lentils
8 cups (4 imperial pints) water
1 large onion, finely chopped
1 clove garlic
¼ cup finely chopped fresh coriander or parsley
⅓ cup (3 fl oz) olive oil
¼ cup (2 fl oz) cold water
1 tablespoon flour
¼ cup (2 fl oz) white vinegar or to taste
salt
freshly ground black pepper

Pick over lentils and wash in several changes of cold water. Drain well. Put lentils in a large pan with 8 cups water, onion, garlic, coriander or parsley (or a combination of the two if preferred), and oil. Bring to the boil, cover pan and simmer on low heat for 1 hour or until lentils are soft. Do not stir while cooking.

Put water and flour in a screw top jar, seal and shake until thoroughly combined. This prevents lumps forming. Pour this gradually into boiling soup, stirring constantly, until thickened slightly. Add vinegar and salt and pepper to taste. Return to the boil, boil gently for 5 minutes and serve hot.

Spanish White Bean Soup

FABADA ASTURIANA

Serves: 6

2 cups (1 lb) large lima beans or other white beans
8 cups (4 imperial pints) water
1 large onion, chopped
3 cloves garlic, finely chopped
250 g (8 oz) salt pork in one piece
250 g (8 oz) laçon (Spanish smoked ham) or proscuitto in one piece
3 smoked chorizo sausages
⅛ teaspoon Spanish saffron powder or 1 teaspoon paprika
salt
freshly ground black pepper

Wash beans well, put in a large pan and add water. Bring to the boil, boil for 2 minutes and remove from heat. Cover and leave for 1 hour or until plump. Return to the boil, add onion and garlic, cover and boil gently on low heat for 30 minutes. Remove skin from pork if present and add to beans with smoked ham. Cook for further hour or until beans are just tender. Rinse sausages, and add to soup with saffron and salt and pepper to taste. Cover and simmer for further 30 minutes. Remove meats and sausages and cut meats into small pieces; slice sausages. Return to soup, heat through and serve in deep plates.

Corn bread is a traditional accompaniment. Though the one preferred in Spain uses yeast for leavening, try the American Mexican-style corn bread on page 99 .

Note: Though the saffron is generally used, even in Spain this expensive spice is replaced with paprika, more for the latter's colour than a flavour substitute.

Italian Bean Soup

Serves: 6

2 cups (1 lb) borlotti beans
8 cups (2 imperial pints) water
1 large onion, finely chopped
½ cup chopped celery
1 bay leaf
salt
freshly ground black pepper
2 cloves garlic, finely chopped
¼ cup (2 fl oz) olive oil
2 tablespoons finely chopped flat leaf parsley

Wash beans, place in a deep pan with 6 cups water and bring to the boil. Boil 2 minutes, remove from heat, cover and leave aside for 2 hours until plump. Add remaining water and return to the boil. Add onion, celery and bay leaf, cover and simmer gently for 2½ hours or until tender. Remove bay leaf and discard. Remove half the beans and mash with potato masher or in food processor. Return to pan and add salt and pepper to taste.

In a frying pan heat oil, add garlic and cook until lightly coloured. Stir in parsley and pour mixture into beans. Bring to the boil on low heat, simmer for 5 minutes and serve in deep plates with crusty bread.

Indian Lentil and Vegetable Soup

SAMBHAR

Serves 6-8

This flavoursome Indian soup is normally flavoured with tamarind, though lemon juice and a little sugar is a good substitute. If you have dried tamarind on hand, soak 1 tablespoon pulp in ½ cup hot water for 10 minutes until soft, break up by rubbing with fingers, then strain through a sieve set over a bowl, rubbing pulp with a spoon. Discard seeds and fibres and use liquid in place of lemon juice and sugar.

1 cup (8 oz) split red lentils or yellow split peas
6 cups (3 imperial pints) water
¼ cup (2 fl oz) oil
1 cup chopped, peeled tomatoes
1 cup diced pumpkin or carrots
1 cup diced young marrow (summer squash)
1 cup chopped green beans or peas
2 teaspoons ground coriander
1 teaspoon ground cummin
½ teaspoon chili powder
2 teaspoons salt or to taste
freshly ground black pepper
1 medium-sized onion, halved lengthwise then sliced
½ teaspoon black mustard seeds
2-3 tablespoons lemon juice
1 teaspoon sugar
boiled rice for serving

Pick over lentils or split peas and wash well. Put in a deep, heavy pan and add the water. Bring to the boil, skimming when necessary. When simmering gently, cover, reduce heat to low and cook until soft — 30 minutes for lentils, 1 hour for split peas.

In a frying pan heat three-quarters of the oil and add all prepared vegetables except onion. Fry on medium heat for 2 minutes, stirring constantly. Stir in coriander, cummin and chili powder and cook for further minute. Pour pan contents into soup. Stir gently to combine and add salt and pepper to taste. Cover and cook gently for further 30 minutes or until vegetables are soft. Wipe out frying pan with paper towels and add remaining oil. Put on medium heat and add sliced onion and mustard seeds. Fry until onion browns and mustard seeds finish popping. Stir into cooked soup, add lemon juice and sugar and leave soup on the heat for a few minutes.

Taste, adjust seasoning, and add a little more lemon juice if necessary. Flavour should be tangy and hot. Serve in small bowls with an accompanying bowl of boiled rice for adding to individual taste.

Very good served with chapatis or rolled up, unfilled dhosai (see index for recipes).

Hungarian Bean Soup

Serves: 6

2 cups (1 lb) cannellini or Great Northern beans
8 cups (4 imperial pints) water
375 g (12 oz) bacon bones or smoked ham hock
2 medium-sized carrots, chopped
1 parsnip, chopped
freshly ground black pepper
2 tablespoons bacon fat
1 small onion, chopped
¼ cup (1 oz) plain flour
2 teaspoons paprika
salt to taste
sour cream for serving

Wash beans well and place in a large pan with the water. Bring to the boil, boil 2 minutes and remove from heat. Cover and leave for 1 hour or until plump. Add rinsed bacon bones or hock, carrots, parsnip and pepper and return to the boil. Cover and simmer on low heat for 1-1½ hours until beans are tender. Remove bones or hock and trim off any meat. Chop finely and return to soup. In a frying pan heat bacon fat, add onion and fry gently until soft. Stir in flour and cook until flour is lightly coloured. Blend about 1½ cups liquid from soup into roux, stirring constantly until thickened. Pour into soup and add paprika and salt to taste. Return to the boil, stirring constantly, reduce heat and simmer gently for 15 minutes. Serve in deep plates with sour cream in a separate bowl to be added to individual taste. Rye or black bread should accompany this soup.

Peruvian Mutton-Red Bean Soup

Serves: 6-8

1½ cups (12 oz) red kidney beans
8 cups (4 imperial pints) water
500g (1lb) mutton or lamb neck, sliced
2 tablespoons butter or oil
1 large onion, chopped
1 clove garlic, crushed
1 large carrot, chopped
1 stalk celery, sliced
250 g (8 oz) ripe tomatoes, chopped
½ cup (4 fl oz) red wine
250 g (8 oz) fresh chorizo sausages
salt
freshly ground black pepper
1 tablespoon chopped parsley

Wash beans well, place in a deep pot and add half the water. Bring to the boil, boil for 2 minutes and remove from heat. Cover and leave for 1 hour until beans are plump. Soak mutton or lamb in salted water for 1 hour, drain and dry with paper towels.

Heat butter or oil in a large frying pan and fry meat on each side until lightly browned. Remove to pot containing soaked beans. To fat remaining in pan add onion and fry gently until soft, add garlic, carrot and celery and fry for 5 minutes. Stir in tomatoes and wine and pour pan contents into beans. Bring slowly to the boil, cover and simmer for 1½ hours until beans are tender. Rinse fresh sausages and add to pot, cover and simmer for further 15 minutes, then add salt and pepper to taste and cook for further 15 minutes.

Remove meat from pot and trim meat off the bones. Chop meat finely and keep aside. Remove sausages, cut in thick slices and put with the meat. Pass soup through a sieve or purée in batches in food processor or blender. Return purée to pot, add meat and sausage pieces and adjust thickness with more water if too thick. Check seasoning. Bring to a slow simmer and serve in large soup plates, sprinkling each serve with chopped parsley. With crusty bread and a good red wine, this makes a satisfying meal.

USING CANNED BEANS: Brown meat and remove to a deep pot. Fry vegetables as directed adding tomatoes and wine. Add to meat with 5 cups water. Cover and simmer for 1½ hours. Add sausages, seasoning and 2 440 g (1 lb) cans undrained red kidney beans. Simmer 15 minutes then finish as above.

Greek Bean Soup, page 24, with the various dried white beans which can be used.

Leek and Butter Bean Soup

Serves: 4–6

1 cup (8 oz) butter or white lima beans
3 cups (1½ imperial pints) water
4 large leeks
¼ cup (2 oz) butter
3 cups (1½ imperial pints) chicken stock
¼ teaspoon ground nutmeg
salt
freshly ground white pepper
¾ cup (6 fl oz) cream
snipped chives for serving

Wash beans well, place in a pan with the water and bring to the boil. Boil for 2 minutes, cover and remove from heat. Leave 2 hours until plump. Return to the boil and boil gently for 1½–2 hours until tender. Beans can be cooked in pressure cooker, following directions on page 10.

Cut off green tops from leeks. Halve white parts lengthwise and wash well, taking care to remove all traces of soil. Slice leeks and put in a pan with the butter. Cook gently until soft without allowing leeks to brown. Add drained beans and chicken stock. Alternatively drain beans, retaining the liquid. Measure this liquid, make up to 3 cups with water and add chicken stock cubes (amount depends on type of cubes – follow directions on pack). Add nutmeg and salt and pepper to taste. Cover and simmer for 15 minutes. Purée in batches in food processor or blender and return to pan. Stir in cream, heat gently without boiling and serve sprinkled with snipped chives.

Mulligatawny

Many versions of this Indian soup exist. The South Indian version is totally vegetarian; the following recipe can be easily adjusted for vegetarian cooking.

1½ cups (12 oz) split red lentils
4 cups (2 imperial pints) water
2 large onions
2 cloves garlic, chopped
2 bay leaves
freshly ground black pepper
3 cups (1½ imperial pints) chicken stock or Vegetable Stock (page 100)
salt
1 tablespoon ghee or oil
1 teaspoon ground turmeric
¼–½ teaspoon chili powder
1 cup thick coconut milk (page 105)
½ teaspoon garam masala
For serving:
boiled rice
lemon wedges

Pick over lentils and wash well. Put in a large pan with the water, bring to the boil, skimming well. Chop 1 onion and add to lentils with 1 chopped garlic clove, bay leaves and a generous grinding of pepper. Cover and simmer for 45 minutes until soft. Purée in food processor or blender, return to pan and add chicken stock, or vegetable stock for vegetarian cooking. Add salt to taste and leave to simmer gently.

Halve remaining onion lengthwise and slice into semicircles. In a frying pan heat ghee or oil and fry onion to a deep golden brown. Stir in remaining garlic, turmeric and chili powder to taste and cook 2 minutes. Blend in coconut milk and garam masala and pour into soup. Stir well and simmer soup gently for 2–3 minutes. Adjust seasoning with more chili powder and salt if necessary. Put a heaped tablespoon of rice in each soup plate and ladle soup over rice. Serve with lemon wedges for squeezing into soup according to individual taste.

Mexican Beans in the Pot, page 43, and Mexican Refried Beans, page 34, with traditional accompaniments.

APPETIZERS AND SNACKS

In Western cooking bean dishes are virtually ignored as taste-tantalizing appetizers or snacks, except, of course, for peanuts — salted, spiced, devilled or whatever. Not so in the cooking of the Middle East and parts of Asia, where meze (appetizers) and snacking are very much a part of daily eating patterns. Creamy, earthy, tangy Hummus scooped up with flat bread; crunchy, flavoursome Falafel or Tameya; and Pakorha, the crisp vegetable fritters of India to name a few.

Today all these are most acceptable to the Western palate, and with modern appliances such as the food processor, are easy to prepare in the Western kitchen.

Chick Pea Pancakes

SOCCA

Makes: 4 pancakes

1 cup (4 oz) chick pea flour (see page 19)
⅔ cup (5 fl oz) cold water
¼ cup (2 fl oz) olive oil
1 teaspoon salt
additional olive oil

Put chick pea flour into a mixing bowl and gradually blend in water using a balloon whisk. Add olive oil and salt and beat until smooth. Cover and leave aside for 1 hour. Brush a 20 cm (8 inch) layer cake pan with olive oil and heat under a hot grill (broiler) for 1 minute. Pour enough batter into hot pan to a depth of 2 mm (⅛ inch) — about ¼ cup. Cook under grill with surface of pancake 10 cm (4 inches) below heat source.

When set and puffing up in places, brush top with olive oil and cook for further 2 minutes until lightly browned. Turn over with pancake turner and cook 1 minute longer. Invert on to a plate, season with salt and pepper and serve hot cut in wedges. Repeat with remaining batter. Cooked socca may be kept warm stacked on a napkin-lined plate, covered with a lid and set over simmering water. Excellent served with drinks as a snack or appetizer.

Egyptian Broad Bean Patties

TAMEYA

Makes: 30

2 cups (1 lb) dried broad beans
water
1 cup chopped spring onions (scallions)
¼ cup chopped parsley
2 tablespoons chopped fresh coriander
3 cloves garlic
1½ teaspoons salt
freshly ground black pepper
¼ teaspoon chili powder
½ teaspoon bicarbonate of soda
2 thick slices stale white bread, crusts removed
sesame seeds, optional
oil for deep frying
For serving:
Arab flat bread
Tahini Sauce (page 108)
salad vegetables

Place beans in a bowl and cover well with cold water. Leave to soak for 2 days, changing water twice each day. Drain beans and remove skins by pressing each firmly with fingers. Bean should pop out, otherwise tear skin with fingernail then squeeze. Pass cleaned beans through food grinder using fine screen. Combine with spring onion, parsley, coriander, garlic, salt, pepper, chili powder and soda. Pass through grinder twice more then knead to a paste. Soak bread in cold water, squeeze thoroughly and crumble into paste. Blend thoroughly and let mixture rest for 30 minutes.

Alternatively all prepared ingredients may be combined and processed in food processor using steel blade. Do this in two batches, then knead well before resting mixture. With wet hands shape about a tablespoon of mixture at a time into thick patties about 4cm (1½ inches) in diameter. Dip each side in sesame seeds if desired. Place on a tray and leave at room temperature for 20 minutes.

Heat oil to 180°C (350°F) or until a cube of bread turns golden in 1 minute. Fry Tameya a few at a time until deep golden brown, turning to brown evenly. Each lot should take 5 minutes to cook. Drain on paper towels. Serve hot with Arab flat bread, Tahini Sauce and assorted salad vegetables such as tomato, cucumber, sweet peppers and lettuce.

Spiced Fried Split Peas

Makes about 2 cups

A popular Indian snack for between meal munching. Have a jar of them on hand and serve as a nibble with drinks.

1 cup (8 oz) yellow split peas
2 cups (1 imperial pint) cold water
1 teaspoon bicarbonate of soda
peanut oil for deep frying
salt
¼–½ teaspoon chili powder
½ teaspoon garam masala

Pick over split peas and wash well in several changes of water. Put into a bowl with the cold water and stir in the soda. Leave in a cool place for 12 hours. Drain, rinse well with cold water and drain again in a sieve, leaving them for an hour or so. Spread onto a tray lined with paper towels and leave to dry.

Heat about 2 cups oil in a saucepan and when hot, but not fuming, pour in about ½ cup of the peas. Fry, stirring often, until golden. Remove with a draining spoon onto paper towels. Repeat until all are fried. An old wire sieve can be used as a frying and draining basket to make this task easier – you will have to bend the handle at right angles so that it can be lowered in with the split peas.

When fried, tip split peas into a bowl and add about 1 teaspoon salt, chili powder to taste and garam masala (an Indian spice mix). Toss well, cool thoroughly and store in an air-tight container until required.

Mexican Refried Beans

FRIJOLES REFRITOS

Serves: 6

1 quantity Frijoles de Olla (page 43)
¼-½ cup lard or oil
For serving:
toasted avocado leaves (page 110)
OR 2 tablespoons chopped fresh coriander
shredded mature cheddar cheese
chopped spring onions (scallions)
warm tortillas

Cook beans as directed but do not remove the cup of beans for mashing. For vegetarian cooking omit bacon bones and replace half the water with vegetable stock (page 100); replace lard with oil.

When beans are very tender, drain off liquid, reserving about 1 cup. Mash beans well with potato masher. Heat ¼ cup lard or oil in a deep frying pan and add mashed beans. Stir over heat until well combined, adding a little bean liquid and additional lard or oil if too dry. Consistency should be similar to creamy mashed potato. Pile into a deep bowl and garnish with crumbled avocado leaves, chopped coriander or spring onions. Serve grated cheese and chopped spring onion in separate bowls; place tortillas in a folded napkin. Bean purée is placed in a tortilla, topped with cheese and onions and rolled up for eating. Chopped tomato, shredded lettuce and taco sauce may also be included as accompaniments.

As an appetiser: Mix 1 cup of the shredded cheese and ½ cup chopped spring onions into the hot beans, pile into a bowl and garnish as desired. Place on a platter and surround with corn chips (fried triangles of tortillas, called tostadas in Mexico, and readily available at Mexican food stores and some delicatessens).

Peanut and Blue Cheese Balls

Makes: About 30

125 g (4 oz) blue vein cheese
250 g (8 oz) packaged cream cheese
1 cup (4 oz) finely chopped, roasted peanuts
2–3 drops Tabasco sauce
1 teaspoon paprika

Break up the blue vein cheese with a fork and place in a small mixer bowl. Soften cream cheese at room temperature and add to bowl. Beat on medium speed until thoroughly combined. Blend in half the peanuts with Tabasco sauce to taste. Add a little salt if necessary, depending on saltiness of cheese. Chill for 1 hour or until firm enough to handle, and shape heaped teaspoons of the mixture into balls.

Put remaining peanuts in a shallow dish and mix in the paprika. Coat balls with this mixture and place on a tray. Chill until required for serving, and serve piled in a bowl as an accompaniment to drinks.

PEANUT AND BLUE CHEESE SPREAD

Make as above, blending all the peanuts into the creamed cheeses. Thin down to a spreading consistency with mayonnaise or cream (or a mixture of the two) and use as a spread on crackers, or to fill crisp celery pieces. The paprika may be omitted, or can be dusted lightly on the finished bowl of spread or on the filled celery.

Dried Bean Patties

FALAFEL

Makes: About 35

1 cup (8 oz) dried broad beans
1 cup (8 oz) chick peas
water
1 medium-sized onion
2 cloves garlic
½ cup finely chopped parsley
pinch hot chili powder
1 teaspoon ground coriander
½ teaspoon ground cummin
1 teaspoon bicarbonate of soda
salt
freshly ground black pepper
oil for deep frying
For serving:
Tahini Cream Sauce (page 108)
Arab flat bread
shredded lettuce
sliced tomato and cucumber

Put broad beans in a bowl and cover with 3 cups cold water. Leave to soak for 48 hours in a cool place, changing water once each day, twice in hot weather. Soak chick peas separately in 3 cups cold water for 12 hours. Drain broad beans and remove skins by pressing firmly — tear skin with fingernail if bean does not pop out. Drain chick peas but do not skin.

Combine beans and peas with roughly chopped onion and garlic and grind twice in food grinder using fine screen, or process in food processor using steel blade. Combine with parsley, chili powder, coriander, cummin and soda and add salt and pepper to taste. Beat well and leave to rest for 1 hour or longer.

Shape a tablespoon of the mixture at a time into balls then flatten into thick patties 4cm (1½ inches) in diameter. Place on a tray and leave for 30 minutes at room temperature. Deep fry in hot oil, 6-8 at a time, and cook for 5-6 minutes turning to brown evenly. When well browned remove and drain on paper towels. Serve hot as an appetiser with Tahini Cream Sauce or as a snack in flat bread, halved and split with the same sauce and salad ingredients.

Note: Skins may be left on the broad beans if desired, but the flavour and texture of the Falafel is much better if removed.

Chick Pea Dip

HUMMUS

Makes: About 3 cups

1 cup chick peas, soaked (page 9)
4 cups (2 imperial pints) water
⅓ cup (3 fl oz) tahini (sesame paste)
¼-½ cup (2-4 fl oz) lemon juice
2 cloves garlic
salt

For serving:
1-2 tablespoons olive oil
chopped parsley
cayenne pepper or paprika
Arab flat bread

Slow or quick soak the chick peas according to directions. Place in a pan, bring to the boil and skim well. Cover and boil gently for 2½ hours or until soft. Alternatively cook in pressure cooker for 20 minutes under pressure (see page 10). Drain liquid and reserve.

Put aside 1 tablespoon of the whole, cooked chick peas for garnish. Purée the remainder of the peas by pressing through a sieve. Skins must be separated for a good hummus. Crush the garlic with one teaspoon salt and beat into purée. Slowly beat in the tahini and lemon juice alternatively. Blend in a little of the reserved liquid to make the mixture a thick creamy consistency. Adjust flavour with salt and lemon to taste.

After puréeing the peas, blending may be completed in food processor or blender. Spread in a shallow dish and swirl with the back of a spoon. Trickle olive oil over the top and garnish with whole chick peas in the centre, chopped parsley around the edge, and a light sprinkling of cayenne or paprika. Serve with Arab flat bread (or crackers).

Salted Roast Chick Peas

Oven Temperature: 150°C (300°F)

A popular nibbling snack in Greece and the Middle East.

1 cup (8 oz) chick peas
cold water
salt

Put chick peas in a bowl and add 3 cups cold water and 1 teaspoon salt. Leave to soak for 10-12 hours. Drain, rinse and spread out on a paper-towel lined tray to dry at room temperature (about 8 hours). Tip into a shallow metal baking dish and sprinkle liberally with strong cooking salt – about 1 tablespoon. Mix through peas with fingertips. Place in a slow oven and roast for 1¼-1½ hours, shaking dish now and then. Cool and store in a screw topped jar.

Fried Dough with Lentils

KOTAH DOLMEH

Makes: 6 dozen

A popular snack in Iran and Afghanistan. Good served hot or warm.

Dough:
1 sachet active dry yeast
1 cup warm water
2 teaspoons rose water
3½ cups plain flour
½ teaspoon salt
¼ teaspoon ground cardamom
¼ cup melted, cooled ghee or oil
Lentil filling:
1 cup (8 oz) brown lentils
3 cups (1½ imperial pints) cold water
2 large onions, finely chopped
⅓ cup (3 oz) ghee
salt
2 tablespoons brown sugar
To finish:
oil for deep frying

Dissolve yeast in ¼ cup warm water, add remaining water and rose water. Sift flour, salt and cardamom into a mixing bowl and remove ½ cup of the flour mixture. Add yeast liquid to flour and mix to a soft dough. Work in ghee or oil with reserved flour, then knead until smooth and elastic – about 10 minutes. Cover and leave in a warm place for 45-60 minutes or until doubled in bulk.

Meanwhile wash lentils well, place in a pan and add cold water. Bring to the boil, cover and simmer over low heat for 1-1¼ hours or until water is absorbed and lentils are soft. Mash with a fork. Gently fry onion in ghee or oil until transparent and lightly browned, add lentils and fry with onion for 5 minutes. Stir in salt to taste and brown sugar. Cool.

Punch down dough and divide into two portions. Roll out each portion thinly to a 45 cm (18 inch) circle. Cut dough into 8 cm (3 inch) rounds with a biscuit cutter and place a generous teaspoon of lentil paste in centre of each round. Moisten edge of dough lightly with water, fold over and press firmly to seal. Press with tines of fork. Beginning with kotah shaped first, deep fry 6-8 at a time for 3 minutes until golden brown and puffed, turning to brown evenly. Lift out with slotted spoon and drain on paper towels. Serve hot or warm as a snack or part of a meal, particularly a picnic meal.

Peanut Cheddar Cheese Pot

250 g (8 oz) tasty mature cheddar cheese
¼ cup (2 oz) butter
2–3 tablespoons dry sherry
½ teaspoon salt
pinch cayenne pepper
½ cup (2 oz) finely chopped, roasted peanuts

Grate cheese coarsely and place in a heavy pan with the butter. Stir over gentle heat until beginning to soften, then stir in 2 tablespoons sherry. Continue to stir over heat until smooth, taking care that it does not over-heat. If mixture becomes oily turn immediately into a bowl. Stir in salt, cayenne and peanuts, whether still in pan or in bowl, and blend in a little more sherry if mixture still has an oily appearance. The cold sherry will cool down the mixture. Taste and adjust seasoning, then transfer to a pottery pot (about 1½ cups in capacity). Smooth top and chill until firm. Serve with crackers or slices of fresh, crusty French bread sticks. Also good served as part of a cheese platter with fruit.

Black-Eyed Bean Fritters

AKARA

Makes: About 60

Known as Akara in Central Africa and Akkra in Jamaica, these hot bean fritters make excellent appetisers. While the African version is highly seasoned and flavoured, Akkra only uses lots of fresh chili and salt.

1 cup (8 oz) black-eyed beans
3 cups (1½ imperial pints) water
2 cloves garlic, chopped
1 small onion
2 teaspoons finely chopped fresh ginger
2 red chilis, seeded and chopped
1½ teaspoons salt
freshly ground black pepper
oil for deep frying

Pick over beans, wash well, put in a bowl with the water and leave to soak in a cool place for at least 6 hours. Drain beans. Put into food processor bowl with steel blade fitted, add chopped garlic, onion, chili and ginger. Process until mixture is light and fluffy — it will be slightly grainy in texture.

Alternatively pass twice through a food grinder fitted with fine screen, then beat with a wooden spoon or electric mixer until light and fluffy. Add salt and pepper to taste. Heat oil in a deep pan or deep fryer and drop in heaped teaspoons of mixture. Fry 6-8 at a time, turning to brown evenly. Cook for 2-3 minutes, remove with a slotted spoon and drain on paper towels. Serve hot. (Fritters can be reheated in a moderate oven for 10 minutes.)

Note: Traditionally the skins of the beans are removed after soaking. Rub handfuls of beans together, then float off loose skins with water. Repeat until beans are skinned. As this is time consuming I have given the easy way out, though I must admit the skinned beans make much better fritters — lighter in texture and more evenly shaped.

Mexican Spiced Peanuts

Makes: About 3 cups
Oven Temperature: 180°C (350°F)

2 tablespoons maize or peanut oil
3 cloves garlic, peeled and left whole
10 dried bird's eye or serrano chilis
1 kg (2 lb) raw shelled peanuts (with outer skin)
1 tablespoon ground sea salt

Put oil in a frying pan with garlic and chilis and place over medium heat. When garlic begins to fry gently add peanuts and cook on medium heat, stirring often. Turn into a large baking dish and sprinkle with the ground salt. Mix through and place in a moderate oven for 30-40 minutes until nuts are roasted without being burnt. Split a nut open — the inside should be just beginning to brown. Tip into another dish to prevent nuts cooking further and leave until cool. Store in a screw top jar for a day or two before serving. When serving, tip quantity required into a dish and pick out any chilis and garlic cloves, returning them to the jar.

Lupini

Lupins are sold in Italian and Middle East stores (called lupini in Italian, troumis in Arabic). Unfortunately few store keepers can tell you how to prepare them – a trap for the uninitiated who might look on them as just another dried bean to try. Point is they cannot be prepared as other beans – the alkaloid content is high, making them bitter. In Italy and some Middle East countries they are sweetened by lengthy processes, ranging from placing the beans in a bag and leaving in a running stream for 2 weeks, to a 12-hour soak, boil, and salt water soak over several days. I have detailed the latter as I doubt if many of you have a fresh, running stream nearby. When prepared the lupins are used as a snack food for nibbling with drinks.

2 cups (1 lb) lupins
water
strong cooking salt

Put lupins in a bowl with about 6 cups cold water and leave in a cool place for 12 hours. Drain off water and rinse. Place in a pan and cover well with fresh water. Bring to the boil and boil gently, covered, for 2 hours or until just tender. (They remain firm-fleshed, so cook until the point of a knife penetrates easily.) Drain again, cover with cold water and leave until cool. Drain and transfer to a bowl, add 6 cups cold water and 2 tablespoons salt. Stir and leave in a cool place (not the refrigerator yet). Twice each day, for the next 6-7 days, drain, rinse and add fresh water and salt.

When lupins taste "sweet" without a trace of bitterness, put into fresh salted water and store in a sealed jar in refrigerator. To serve take out what is required, drain well and serve plain or with a squeeze of lemon juice. Skins may be eaten or discarded.

Egyptian Brown Bean Purée

FUL MEDAMIS

Serves: 6–8

The national dish of Egypt, sold morning, noon and deep into the night by the 'ful' vendors. Though regarded as a snack, and eaten as such, a bowl of ful medamis is often served as a meal with hard boiled eggs and salad accompaniment. This is the snack version.

2 cups (1 lb) Egyptian brown beans (ful)
¼ cup (2 oz) split red lentils
4 cups (2 imperial pints) water
salt
3 cloves garlic
¼ teaspoon ground cummin
freshly ground black pepper
2–3 tablespoons lemon juice
¼ cup (2 fl oz) olive oil
2 tablespoons chopped parsley
Arab flat bread

Wash beans well and place in a heavy pan with the water. Bring to the boil, boil 2 minutes and remove from heat. Cover and leave for 1 hour or until plump. Alternatively beans may be slow-soaked overnight following directions on page 9 – drain and add fresh water. Add washed lentils to beans and bring to the boil. Skim well, cover tightly and simmer very gently without stirring for 4–5 hours until soft. Beans may be cooked in pressure cooker after plumping, following directions on page 10.

Crush garlic with 1 teaspoon salt and stir into beans with cummin and pepper to taste. Purée in batches in food processor or blender, turn into a bowl and beat in lemon juice to taste and the olive oil. Adjust seasoning with salt and pepper. Serve warm or at room temperature spread on a serving dish and sprinkled with parsley. Purée is scooped up with pieces of flat bread. Additional lemon wedges can be on hand for those who like to add more.

Soya Bean Pancakes

Makes: About 16

This uses the residue left after making bean curd (see page 103). If you choose not to make the bean curd, just soak soya beans overnight, drain, rinse and grind to a paste in food processor. Do not use any water when grinding. Either the residue or the ground, soaked beans will keep in a sealed container in refrigerator for 2 days.

2 cups ground soaked soya beans
1 cup (4 oz) plain flour
2 teaspoons baking powder
¼ cup (2 oz) caster (fine) sugar
2 eggs, beaten
butter for cooking

Place ground soya beans in a bowl. Sift flour with baking powder and add to bean paste with sugar. Blend thoroughly. Beat eggs in cup measure and make up to 1 cup with milk. Beat into bean mixture with a wooden spoon, adding a little more milk to make a thick batter. Heat a griddle or large frying pan and grease with a wad of paper towel dipped in butter. Pour about 2 tablespoons of mixture onto hot surface forming pancakes about 10 cm (4 inches) in diameter. Spread out with back of spoon. When small bubbles appear on top surface and base is brown, turn with pancake turner and cook other side. Stack on a napkin-lined plate and keep warm until all are cooked. Serve hot with butter and maple or golden syrup, or honey. A very nourishing breakfast or snack.
Note: If beginning from scratch soak ¾ cup soya beans in plenty of water. Rinse well and drain.

Chick Pea Balls

FELAFEL

Makes: About 25

Though similar in name, these chick pea balls are quite different to the Lebanese Falafel. This is an Israeli version indigenous to the region. The burghul used in the recipe is now widely available in health food stores as well as Middle Eastern food stores. A fine or coarse grade burghul can be used.

1 cup (8 oz) chick peas
3 cups (1½ imperial pints) water
½ cup (4 oz) burghul (steamed cracked wheat)
1 cup (½ imperial pint) boiling water
2 cloves garlic, chopped
2 tablespoons chopped parsley
1 teaspoon baking powder
¼ cup plain flour
1 teaspoon ground coriander
1 teaspoon ground cummin
¼ teaspoon chili powder
3 teaspoons lemon juice
2 teaspoons salt
freshly ground black pepper
oil for deep frying
For serving:
Tahini Cream Sauce (page 108)
Arab flat bread, optional
salad vegetables, optional

Wash chick peas and cover with the water. Leave to soak for 12–15 hours in a cool place. Soak burghul in the boiling water for 10 minutes and drain in a fine sieve, pressing well with the back of a spoon to extract moisture.

Drain chick peas, mix in garlic and parsley and pass through food grinder using fine screen. Mix burghul into ground mixture and pass again through grinder. Alternatively chick peas, garlic, parsley and burghul may be processed in food processor using steel blade. Process to a coarse paste.

Blend in baking powder, flour, coriander, cummin, chili powder, lemon juice, salt and pepper to taste. With moistened hands shape into balls the size of a walnut. Place on a tray and leave for 30 minutes.

Deep fry 6–7 at a time in hot oil, cooking them for 5 minutes. Turn to brown evenly. Drain on paper towels and serve as an appetizer with the Tahini Cream Sauce. As a snack, serve 2–3 felafel in the pocket of halved flat bread, add shredded lettuce, sliced tomatoes, cucumber and sweet green pepper, and spoon on some Tahini Cream Sauce.

Broad Bean Purée

BESARA

Serves: 6

Though regarded as an Egyptian dish, this purée is also popular in Italy, and often fed to children as a nourishing, light meal flavoured with olive oil and lemon juice, but without the fried onion garnish and raw onion accompaniment.

2 cups (1 lb) broad beans (see page 15)
6 cups (3 imperial pints) cold water
salt
freshly ground black pepper
2 teaspoons dried mint leaves
2 medium-sized onions
¼ cup (2 fl oz) olive oil
2 cloves garlic, finely chopped
For serving:
additional olive oil, optional
chopped onions
lemon wedges
crusty or Arab flat bread

Soak broad beans in water to cover for 48 hours, changing water twice each day. Leave in a cool place while soaking. Drain beans and remove tough skin from beans. If you can find dried broad beans without the skin, then simply soak 1½ cups of these beans for 12 hours.

Put skinned beans and measured amount of water in pan (preferably not aluminium) and bring to the boil. Cover and simmer gently for 1½ hours or until very soft. Purée in batches in food processor or blender and return to pan. Add salt and pepper to taste, and mint rubbed to a powder. Leave to simmer gently for a few minutes. Meanwhile halve peeled onion lengthwise and slice into semicircles. Heat olive oil in a frying pan and add onion. Fry until golden brown, add garlic and cook 1 minute. Remove from heat.

Put purée into small dishes and garnish each with the fried onion and oil mixture. Serve with a cruet of olive oil, chopped onion and lemon wedges for adding to individual taste. Have plenty of bread on hand for scooping up purée.

Vegetables in Chick Pea Batter

PAKORHA

Serves: 6-8

Batter:
1½ cups (6 oz) chick pea flour (besan) or lentil flour
¾ cup (6 fl oz) cold water
1 clove garlic, crushed
½ teaspoon ground coriander
½ teaspoon tumeric
¼ teaspoon ground cummin
⅛ teaspoon chili powder
¼ teaspoon baking powder
1½ teaspoons salt or to taste
Vegetables:
1 small eggplant
½ small cauliflower
2 small potatoes
1 large onion
To finish:
oil for deep frying

Put chick pea flour into a mixing bowl, add half the water and stir until smooth. Gradually add remaining water, beating well. Stir in garlic, spices, baking powder and salt. Cover and leave aside for at least 1 hour.

Wash eggplant, dry and cut into chunky pieces with skin on. Sprinkle liberally with salt and leave aside for 30 minutes. Dry well with paper towels.

Wash cauliflower and break into small florets, cutting thicker florets in halves or quarters. Cook in boiling, salted water for 3 minutes. Drain, rinse in cold water, place on paper towels to dry. Peel potatoes and slice thinly. Soak in cold water for 20 minutes, drain and dry. Peel onion and cut out root. Cut onion into 6 wedges and separate leaves. As centre sections will be small, keep aside for another use.

Beat batter for a few seconds, adding a little water if too thick. Heat oil in a deep frying pan until a drop of batter rises immediately to the surface. Dip vegetable pieces into batter and fry about 6 pieces at a time, turning them to brown evenly. Each batch should cook in 4-5 minutes, long enough to cook the vegetables without burning the batter. Lift out with a slotted spoon and drain on paper towels. Serve hot as a snack or appetiser. Natural yoghurt or a fruit chutney may be used as a dipping sauce.

Fried Bean Curd

Serves: 6–8

8 squares bean curd
3 teaspoons salt
½ teaspoon freshly ground black pepper
peanut oil for frying
2 tablespoons soya sauce

Rinse bean curd gently in cold water and place on a clean cloth spread in a flat dish, spacing pieces well apart. Fold cloth over bean curd to cover it and put a flat board on top. Weigh down evenly with a heavy object and leave until compressed to half original thickness – about 2 hours. In hot weather it is best to put it in the refrigerator. When compressed cut each square into quarters.

Heat salt in a dry frying pan or wok until lightly coloured. Stir in pepper and remove from heat. Pour into a small bowl or tiny dishes and keep aside.

Heat about 3 cups oil in a wok or deep frying pan until very hot. Briefly dip a large, flat frying ladle (wire or perforated metal) into oil, lift out and place a few squares of bean curd on it. Return to oil and fry until golden brown. Drain on paper towels, transfer to serving dish and keep warm while remainder is fried. Sprinkle bean curd with soya sauce and serve with the salt and pepper mixture so that pieces may be seasoned to individual taste.

BEANFEASTS

If we are to believe what we see on the silver screen, the American West was won on plates of beans; the term 'beanfeast' or 'beano' refers to the annual English employer's dinner for his employees where beans and bacon were considered an essential dish.

And while you may not consider canned baked beans as a feast, to the impoverished, it certainly was and is. So it seems beans have earned the reputation of being a low cost, nourishing food, but this does not mean that they have to be regaled to lowly ranks. A bean dish can feed a hungry family, extend the meat, be served with pride to guests, and your reputation as a cook will soar.

Mexican Beans in the Pot

FRIJOLES DE OLLA

Serves: 6

2 cups (1 lb) pinto, black or pink beans
6 cups (3 imperial pints) cold water
125 g (4 oz) bacon bones
¼ cup (2 oz) lard
1 large onion, chopped
salt
freshly ground black pepper
2 tablespoons chopped fresh coriander or 1 teaspoon dried oregano leaves
For serving:
finely chopped spring onions (scallions)
sour cream
mild pickled peppers or fresh mild pepper strips

Wash beans well, put in a bowl with the water. Soak for 6-8 hours in a cool place. Alternatively pinto or pink beans may be quick soaked – bring to the boil, boil 2 minutes, cover and leave aside for 1-2 hours until plump. Bring beans and their soaking water to the boil, cover and simmer gently for 1 hour. Add rinsed bacon bones, cover and cook until tender, about 1 hour longer for pink beans, 1½ hours for pintos, 3 hours for black beans.

Add more water to pan when necessary to keep beans just covered in liquid. Heat lard in a frying pan and add chopped onion. Fry until lightly browned. Add to beans with salt and pepper to taste, cover and simmer for 15 minutes longer. Remove bacon bones. Remove about 1 cup beans with some liquid to a bowl and mash well. Stir into beans in pan, then serve in small bowls with accompaniments served in separate bowls to be added according to taste.

For vegetarian cooking: Omit bacon bones and replace 3 cups water with unsalted vegetable stock (page 100). Use oil instead of lard.

Chili Con Carne

Serves: 6

1 cup (8 oz) red kidney beans
3 cups (1½ imperial pints) water
1 small sweet green pepper
750 g (1½ lb) chuck or skirt (flank) steak
2 tablespoons lard or oil
1 large onion, chopped
2 cloves garlic, crushed
425 g (1 lb) can tomatoes, chopped
1 teaspoon ground coriander
½ teaspoon ground cummin
½-1 teaspoon chili powder
salt
freshly ground black pepper
2 tablespoons chopped fresh coriander
For serving:
corn bread (page 98) or
corn tortillas

Wash kidney beans well, put into a pan with the water and bring to the boil. Boil 2 minutes, remove from heat, cover and leave for 1 hour until plump. Return to the boil and simmer gently for 1½ hours or until just tender. Clean the pepper, cut into quarters and coarsely grate the flesh. Cut meat into 1 cm (½ inch) cubes. Heat lard or oil in a deep frying pan with lid to fit and brown beef quickly in two lots. Remove to a plate. Add onion to pan and fry gently until transparent. Add garlic and grated pepper and fry for 1 minute.

Return meat to pan with tomatoes, ground coriander and cummin and add chili powder, salt and pepper to taste. Cover and simmer gently for 1 hour, adding a little of the bean liquid if too dry. Drain beans reserving liquid, and add beans to pan. Cover and cook for further 30 minutes, adding more bean liquid if necessary. Mixture should be moist, but not too liquid. When beans and meat are tender, stir in chopped coriander and serve with warm corn bread or warm corn tortillas if available.

USING CANNED BEANS: Replace cooked dried beans with 1 675 g (1½ lb) or 2 300 g (10 oz) cans red kidney beans.

Black Beans with Garlic

Serves: 6

2 cups (1 lb) Mexican black beans
6 cups (3 imperial pints) water
salt to taste
1 tablespoon lard or oil
125 g (4 oz) salt pork
3 cloves garlic, finely sliced
1 teaspoon cummin seed

Wash beans well and place in a pan with the water. Bring to the boil, remove from heat, cover and leave for 1 hour. Return to the boil and boil gently for 2 hours or until beans are tender and still intact. Add salt to taste after 1½ hours cooking. Drain beans when cooked and keep hot. Remove skin from salt pork if present and discard. Cut pork into 1 cm (½ inch) dice.

Heat a heavy frying pan and add lard and pork. Fry on medium high heat, stirring often, until brown and crisp. Add garlic slices and fry a few seconds until golden brown. Add cummin seed, cook a few seconds longer, then add beans and stir gently over heat for 2-3 minutes. Serve immediately with wholemeal bread.

Note: Pinto or red kidney beans may be prepared in the same way – adjust bean cooking time accordingly.

Chick Peas With Meats

COCIDO

Serves: 8-10

This famous Spanish dish is usually served in three separate courses – soup, vegetables, then meats. I prefer it as two – soup then a meat and vegetable platter. Many regional versions of Cocido exist; this version was given to me by a Spanish friend from Asturiana.

2 cups (1 lb) chick peas, soaked (see page 9)
8 cups (4 imperial pints) water
1 kg (2 lb) lean fresh beef brisket in one piece
250 g (8 oz) salt pork, skin removed
500 g (1 lb) laçon (smoked Spanish ham) or proscuitto
2 cloves garlic, crushed
1 medium-sized onion, peeled
500 g (1 lb) medium-sized carrots, scraped
2 cm (¾ inch) square unto (page 105), optional
500 g (1 lb) smoked chorizo sausages
1 small roasting chicken, about 1 kg (2 lb)
salt
freshly ground black pepper
6 small potatoes, peeled
½ white cabbage cut in 6 wedges
1 cup crushed vermicelli noodles
Aioli (page 104), optional

Wash chick peas well and slow or quick soak with 6 cups water. Bring to the boil in a large pot, cover and boil gently for 1½ hours. Add remaining water with beef brisket, scalded salt pork, laçon or proscuitto, garlic, whole onion and quartered carrots. Return slowly to the boil, skimming well. When boiling gently, cover and simmer for 1½ hours. Add the whole chorizos and the whole chicken, cover and simmer for further 30 minutes. Season to taste with salt and pepper and add whole potatoes. Cover and cook for further 30-45 minutes until meats are tender and potatoes cooked. Put cabbage wedges carefully on top of meats, cover and simmer for 15 minutes.

Carefully drain off liquid into another pan, bring to the boil and add the vermicelli. Boil rapidly for 10 minutes. Serve soup in a tureen as the first course. Arrange carved meats, chicken and sliced sausages on a platter and surround with carrots, potatoes and cabbage. Serve chick peas in a separate bowl with any remaining liquid from pot. Aioli, though not traditional, is an excellent accompaniment.

Carbonade of Rabbit and Beans

Serves: 5–6

2 cups (1 lb) cannellini or Great Northern beans
6 cups (3 imperial pints) water
salt to taste
1 rabbit, about 1 kg (2 lb)
2 tablespoons olive oil
2 tablespoons butter
2 large onions, chopped
2 cloves garlic, crushed
1½ cups (12 fl oz) beer
¼ teaspoon ground nutmeg
3 teaspoons brown sugar
freshly ground black pepper
1 bay leaf

Wash beans and quick soak according to directions on page 9. When plump return to the boil and boil for 30 minutes. Drain.

Joint rabbit and soak in salted water for 1 hour. Drain and dry. Heat butter and oil in a deep pan and brown rabbit on all sides. Remove to a plate. Add onion to pan and fry gently until soft, add garlic, cook a few seconds and pour in beer. Stir in nutmeg, sugar, add salt and pepper to taste and bay leaf.

Return rabbit to pan, add partly cooked beans, cover and simmer for 1½ hours until rabbit and beans are tender. Add some water if necessary, but rabbit juices will add to liquid content during cooking. Remove bay leaf and serve with a green vegetable.

Boston Baked Beans

Serves: 6-8
Oven Temperature: 130°C (275°F)

3 cups (1½ lb) haricot (navy) beans
8 cups (4 imperial pints) water
250 g (8 oz) salt pork
⅓ cup (3 fl oz) dark treacle or molasses
2 tablespoons brown sugar
1 teaspoon dry mustard
1 small onion, grated
salt to taste

Wash beans well, put in a pan with the water and bring to the boil. Boil 2 minutes, cover and leave off heat for 1 hour, until plump. Return to the boil and boil for 30 minutes. Drain, reserving liquid. Scald salt pork with boiling water, drain and cut into two pieces. Score skin with a sharp knife. Place half the beans in a bean pot or casserole dish and put one piece of pork on top. Add remaining beans and push second piece of pork into beans, leaving skin partly exposed. Heat 1½ cups bean liquid and stir in treacle or molasses. Blend brown sugar with mustard, breaking up lumps and stir into liquid with onion. Pour over beans, adding more bean liquid if necessary to cover beans. Cover and cook in a very slow oven for 6 hours. Stir gently each 2 hours, adding more liquid if beans look dry. After 6 hours add salt to taste, cover and cook for further hour or until beans are soft. Remove lid and cook uncovered for 30 minutes. Take out pork and cut into small pieces. Mix into beans and serve with fried tiny chipolata sausages.

BAKED BEANS IN TOMATO SAUCE
Follow ingredients and method for Boston Baked Beans, replacing salt pork with a 125 g (4 oz) piece of smoked bacon, scalding the bacon and scoring skin, but leaving it in one piece. After 6 hours add ½ cup tomato sauce (catsup) to beans with 1 teaspoon Worcestershire Sauce and salt. Cover and cook for further hour or until tender, remove lid and cook uncovered for 20 minutes or until beans are soft and sauce is thick. Remove bacon, chop finely and stir into beans.

Moroccan Chicken and Chick Peas, page 59.

Cassoulet

Serves: 10-12
Oven Temperature: 200°C (400°F) reducing to 150°C (300°F)

A classic French dish made with a variety of preserved and fresh meats ever-present in the French farmhouse kitchen. The beans add substance and absorb the delicious combination of flavours during the long, slow cooking. A piece of preserved goose is often added, and though fresh chicken or duck might do as a substitute, the dish is just as delicious without either of these meats. Serve it to a crowd for a real beanfeast.

I have given alternatives to meats so that you may adjust ingredients according to availability and to suit your pocket.

4 cups (2 lb) haricot (navy) beans, soaked (page 9)
250 g (8 oz) fresh pork skin (rind)
2 large onions
1 carrot, scraped
bouquet garni (2 sprigs each thyme and parsley, 1 bay leaf, leafy top of 1 celery stalk)
3 cloves garlic, crushed
½ small leg lamb or 750 g (1½ lb) lamb breast
375 g (12 oz) salt pork or bacon, in 1 piece
375 g (12 oz) fresh or smoked garlic sausage (chorizos are ideal and easily obtained)
1 small chicken or duck, optional
2 large ripe tomatoes, peeled and chopped
salt
freshly ground black pepper
¼ cup soft white breadcrumbs
chopped parsley to garnish

Either slow or quick soak beans according to basic directions. Place in a large pot with soaking liquid. Cut pork skin into small squares and add to beans with 1 onion, quartered carrot, bouquet garni and 2 cloves garlic. Bring to the boil, skim well, then cover and boil gently for 1 hour or until beans are tender but still intact. Remove onion, carrot and bouquet garni. Drain beans, reserving liquid.

While beans are cooking, put lamb, salt pork or bacon, sausages and chicken or duck (if used) in a roasting dish and roast in hot oven for 30 minutes. Cut lamb into cubes, salt pork or bacon and sausages into slices, chicken or duck into small pieces on the bone. Meats should be browned but not completely cooked. Keep the fat in the dish.

Place a layer of beans and pork skin in a large casserole dish and top with a mixture of the meat, sausage and poultry pieces. Repeat until all these ingredients are used. Chop remaining onion and add to fat in roasting dish. Place over heat and sauté gently until transparent. Add remaining garlic and cook for a few seconds, then add chopped tomatoes and 3 cups bean liquid. Bring to the boil, scraping any juices in dish. Pour over casserole contents and add salt and pepper to taste. Cover and cook in a slow oven for 1½ hours, adding more bean liquid if necessary. Remove lid and sprinkle top with one-third of the crumbs.

Cook until fat and crumbs form a crust, stir this through the beans and add remaining crumbs. Cook again until a crust forms, stir through again and repeat a third time. By this time all ingredients should be tender. Sprinkle with chopped parsley and serve with a tossed green salad on the side and crusty bread.

Note: A combination of smoked, cured and fresh meats give the characteristic flavour. If salt pork is used, then use smoked garlic flavoured sausages; if bacon is preferred, use fresh sausages.

Dutch Brown Beans and Bacon, page 50.

Pease Pudding with Salt Pork

Serves: 6

An old English favourite, and a hearty meal for sharp winter appetites. While a hand of salt pork or a piece of boiling bacon is used in England, the only salt pork readily available in the United States is the sparerib. As this is too fatty, have meat retailer salt a fresh shoulder picnic, or use smoked pork shoulder picnic.

1 hand salt pork or 1 kg (2 lb) piece of boiling bacon
water
2 small whole onions
3 large carrots, quartered
3 parsnips, quartered
1 stick celery, cut in 4 pieces
½ teaspoon whole peppercorns

Pease Pudding:
2 cups (1 lb) yellow split peas
1 large onion, chopped
¼ cup (2 oz) butter
salt to taste
freshly ground black pepper
2 eggs, beaten

Soak salt pork in cold water for 1 hour; boiling bacon should be soaked overnight. Drain meat and place in a deep pan. Cover with cold water and bring to the boil, skimming as required. When well skimmed and simmering, add vegetables and peppercorns, cover and simmer gently for 1½ hours or until meat is almost tender.

While meat is cooking, wash peas well, place in a heavy pan with 4 cups (2 imperial pints) cold water. Bring to the boil, skim well and add chopped onion. Reduce heat, cover and simmer for 1½ hours or until very soft. Do not stir during cooking. Purée with a potato masher and stir over heat to dry the purée a little. It should hold its shape when stirred. Blend in butter and salt and pepper to taste. Cool a little, then stir in beaten eggs. Flour a scalded cloth; pile mixture in centre and tie securely. Put into pan with gently boiling meat and cook for further 30 minutes. Turn pease pudding onto serving dish. Lift out meat, carve and arrange on one side, place vegetables on other side and serve.

Dutch Brown Beans and Bacon

Serves: 4-6

2 cups (1 lb) brown beans, soaked (page 9)
8 cups (4 imperial pints) water
salt
250 g (8 oz) smoked speck or other smoked fatty bacon
1 large onion
4-6 dill-pickled cucumbers

Wash beans well and slow soak as directed. Drain, place in a pan and add the water. Bring to the boil, cover and boil gently for 2½-3 hours until tender, adding salt to taste after 2 hours cooking.

Cut speck or bacon in 5 mm (¼ inch) slices, then cut each slice in 2 cm (¾ inch) squares. Heat a heavy frying pan and add speck. Fry until browned. Remove with a slotted spoon, leaving fat in pan. Halve onion lengthwise, then slice across into semi-circles. Fry in fat until lightly browned.

Drain beans and place in a warm dish. Pour onion and fat over beans, and put speck on top. Cut pickled cucumbers into quarters lengthwise and arrange around edge of dish. Serve hot.

Spiced Soya Bean Patties

Serves: 6

As any soya bean recipe is usually prepared as a meat substitute rather than in any traditional way, I devised this version giving them an Asian flavour. At first I cooked it as a loaf, but results were disappointing. When cooked as patties or rissoles, they make a very acceptable meat substitute.

1½ cups (12 oz) soya beans
6 cups water
salt to taste
1 large onion, finely chopped
2 tablespoons oil
1 clove garlic
1 teaspoon grated fresh ginger
1 tablespoon finely chopped sweet green pepper
1 tablespoon finely chopped sweet red pepper
1 egg
½ cup (1 oz) soft wholemeal breadcrumbs
⅛ teaspoon chili powder
freshly ground black pepper
4 teaspoons soya sauce
1 teaspoon brown sugar
2 tablespoons finely chopped fresh coriander
To finish:
plain flour
1 egg, beaten
dried breadcrumbs
oil for shallow frying

Wash beans well, put in a pan with the water and bring to the boil. Boil 2 minutes, remove from heat, cover and leave for 1 hour until plump. Drain and add 6 cups fresh water. Bring to the boil and simmer, covered, for 4 hours or until tender. Add salt to taste after 3 hours and add more water if necesary during cooking. (These may be cooked a day or two before required, drained and refrigerated in a covered container.)

Mash drained beans well with potato masher or in food processor and turn into a bowl. In a pan sauté onion until soft, add garlic and ginger and cook a few seconds. Add to beans with egg, soft breadcrumbs, chopped peppers, chili powder, pepper, soy sauce, brown sugar and chopped coriander. Mix well, adding salt to taste. Shape generous tablespoons of mixture into balls with moistened hands. Roll in flour and flatten into thick patties. Brush with beaten egg and coat with breadcrumbs. Shallow-fry in hot oil until golden brown on each side. Drain on paper towels and serve hot with accompanying vegetables.

USING CANNED BEANS: Replace cooked dried beans with 3 300 g (10 oz) cans soya beans, heated and drained.

Lentil Beef Loaf

Serves: 5–6
Oven temperature: 180°C (350°F)

½ cup (4 oz) split red lentils
1 cup (½ imperial pint) water
1 medium-sized onion
1 tablespoon oil
1 small clove garlic, crushed
2 teaspoons curry powder
500 g (1 lb) finely ground beef
½ teaspoon grated lemon rind
1 egg
salt
freshly ground black pepper

Pick over lentils, wash well and place in a pan with the water. Bring to the boil, skim well, then reduce heat and cover pan. Cook gently without stirring for 30 minutes or until lentils are soft and water is absorbed. Turn into a bowl and cool.

Chop onion very finely and fry gently in oil in a frying pan. When transparent add garlic and curry powder and cook 2 minutes, stirring often. Pour onto lentils and mix through. Blend in remaining ingredients, adding salt and pepper to taste. Pack into a greased loaf pan.

Grease a slab cake pan or oven-proof dish and invert loaf pan onto this. Meat loaf will release itself during cooking. Cook in a moderate oven for 30 minutes, remove loaf tin and brush loaf with oil. Leave in oven for 10 minutes to brown lightly. Let loaf stand 5 minutes before slicing to serve. A fruit chutney goes well with this loaf, and serve with vegetable accompaniment.

Crab in Black Bean Sauce

Serves: 4

This is not a recipe for the squeamish, as the crabs must be alive just before cooking. I shan't go into the gory details of how an expert Chinese cook might do this, as I prefer to put the crab into the freezer for 10 minutes to immobilise it, then bravely chop the poor creature in half with a blow of the cleaver. As the crab is usually tied securely when purchased, scrub the shell well before it goes into the freezer (or suffers another fate).

2 fresh crabs, each about 500 g (1 lb)
2 tablespoons salted black beans
2 cloves garlic, crushed
1 teaspoon finely chopped fresh ginger
¼ cup (2 fl oz) peanut oil
1 red chili, seeded and chopped finely
2 teaspoons sugar
4 spring onions (scallions), sliced diagonally
¾ cup (6 fl oz) water
2 teaspoons cornflour

Scrub and immobilize crab. Chop in half with a cleaver or heavy knife and clean out grey fibrous tissue and stomach bag. Rinse and chop body into 4 pieces, leaving legs attached. Remove large claws and crack in several places with flat side of cleaver; crack legs lightly.

Soak dry salted beans in cold water for 10 minutes; if using canned beans rinse under cold water. Drain well and put into a bowl with garlic and ginger. Mash to a paste with a fork.

Heat oil in a wok or frying pan and add chili and crab pieces. Stir-fry until crab turns red. Add black bean mixture and stir-fry for further 2 minutes, then sprinkle in sugar. Mix cornfour with the water and pour into pan, stirring pan contents until liquid thickens and coats crab pieces. Cover and simmer for 2 minutes, add spring onions, stir well then serve immediately.

Chicken Satays

Serves: 6

1 kg (2 lb) chicken breasts
1 tablespoon tamarind pulp (page 18)
¼ cup (2 fl oz) hot water
2 medium-sized onions
2 cloves garlic
2 teaspoons chopped fresh ginger
1 teaspoon ground coriander
1 teaspoon ground cummin
1 teaspoon ground turmeric
3 teaspoons brown sugar
peanut oil for basting
For serving:
Peanut Sauce (page 103)
boiled rice
cucumber chunks

Bone chicken breasts and remove skin. Cut flesh into 2 cm (¾ inch) cubes and place in a glass bowl. Soak tamarind in hot water and strain as directed on page 18. Put roughly chopped onions, garlic and ginger in food processor or blender and grind finely. Blend in coriander, cummin, turmeric, brown sugar and tamarind liquid. Pour over chicken, stir well, cover and leave in refrigerator to marinate for 3 hours or longer, stirring occasionally. Soak 6 bamboo skewers in cold water for several hours.

When required for cooking, drain chicken and thread onto bamboo skewers. Brush with oil and cook over glowing charcoal or under a pre-heated griller (broiler), turning and basting frequently with oil. Do not cook with too fierce a heat as chicken will toughen. Serve hot with Peanut Sauce, boiled rice and chunks of crisp cucumber.

Steamed Fish-Black Bean Sauce

Serves: 4

1 whole fish (snapper, bream, bass) about 1 kg (2 lb)
salt
½ teaspoon grated fresh ginger
2 tablespoons salted black beans
2 tablespoons dry sherry
1 teaspoon brown vinegar
1 teaspoon sugar
½ teaspoon sesame oil
3 spring onions (scallions) sliced diagonally, including some green tops

Scale and clean fish, rinse and pat dry. Leave whole. Rub cavity and outside surfaces with salt and grated ginger. Leave aside.

If dry salted black beans are used, soak in cold water for 10 minutes. Canned beans need only be rinsed under cold water. Drain beans, place in a bowl and mash to a paste. Stir in sherry, vinegar and sugar.

Take a heatproof plate large enough to take fish and rub with sesame oil. Put fish on plate and pour over black bean mixture. Cover and leave aside for 30 minutes.

In a fish steamer or large wok fitted with a rack, add water to come just below rack and bring to the boil. Sprinkle half the spring onion over the fish and cover with a lid to fit or use foil; pressing it securely over plate rim. Place on rack, cover steamer or wok and steam for 20-25 minutes, depending on thickness of fish. Remove cover, garnish with remaining spring onion and serve immediately with boiled rice. Stir-fried Bean Sprouts (see Index) is a good accompaniment.

Shami Kebabs

Serves: 6

A favourite from the Middle East to India, each region having its own particular spicing. This version is from the Arabian Gulf States. Use canned chick peas for convenience, or cook your own.

2 cups cooked chick peas
500 g (1 lb) finely minced lean beef or lamb
1 medium-sized onion, grated
¼ teaspoon ground cummin
½ teaspoon ground coriander
⅛ teaspoon chili powder
¼ teaspoon ground cardamom, optional
pinch each ground clove and nutmeg
½ teaspoon freshly ground black pepper
salt to taste
2 tablespoons finely chopped flat leaf parsley
oil for frying

Drain chick peas and purée in food processor or pass through food grinder using fine screen. Blend into meat with onion, spices, seasonings and parsley. Knead by hand until thoroughly combined and paste-like in consistency. Moisten hands and shape generous tablespoons of the mixture into thick, 4 cm (1½ inch) patties. Shallow fry in hot oil over medium-high heat for about 3-4 minutes each side. Drain on paper towels and serve hot with vegetables or cold with salad.

Stir-Fried Pork and Bean Sprouts

Serves: 4-5

- **500 g (1 lb) lean pork loin**
- **2 tablespoons salted black beans**
- **1 red chili, seeded and chopped**
- **1 clove garlic, crushed**
- **1 teaspoon finely chopped fresh ginger**
- **4 spring onions (scallions) sliced diagonally**
- **1 cup (4 oz) bean sprouts**
- **2 tablespoons peanut oil**
- **1 tablespoon soya sauce**
- **1 tablespoon dry sherry**
- **2 teaspoons sugar**
- **2 teaspoons cornflour**
- **½ cup (4 fl oz) chicken stock**

Heat oil in a wok or frying pan and stir-fry pork strips on high heat until lightly browned. Add black bean mixture and stir-fry for 1 minute, then add spring onions and bean sprouts and stir-fry for further minute. Combine soy sauce, sherry, sugar, cornflour and chicken stock, pour into pork mixture and stir over heat until thickened and bubbling. Serve immediately with boiled rice.

Slice pork into very thin strips about 5 cm (2 inches) long. If dry salted black beans are used, soak in cold water for 10 minutes; rinse canned black beans under cold water. Drain beans and mash well with a fork. Combine with chili, garlic and ginger. Prepare spring onions, including some of the green tops. Rinse bean sprouts under cold water, drain and remove any skins and brown tips.

Spiced Peanut Chicken

Serves: 5–6

A chicken stew from Indonesia, where peanuts feature prominently in cooking. If you like a hotter flavour, increase the chili powder or add 2 red chilis, seeded and finely chopped, when frying the onions.

- **1.5 kg (3 lb) chicken pieces**
- **2 cloves garlic, crushed**
- **1 teaspoon grated fresh ginger**
- **1½ teaspoons ground coriander**
- **1 teaspoon ground cummin**
- **⅛–¼ teaspoon chili powder**
- **1 teaspoon ground turmeric**
- **1 teaspoon salt**
- **½ cup (2 oz) ground, roasted peanuts**
- **2 tablespoons peanut oil**
- **1 large onion, chopped**
- **½ cup (4 fl oz) thick coconut milk (page 105)**
- **½ cup (4 fl oz) water**
- **thinly peeled strip lemon rind**
- **5 cm (2 inch) piece cinnamon bark**
- **2 teaspoons brown sugar**
- **3 teaspoons dark soya sauce**
- **1 tablespoon lemon juice**

For serving:

Spiced Peanuts and Coconut (page 105), optional

Cut chicken pieces into serving portions if too large and wipe dry. Combine garlic with ginger, coriander, cummin, chili powder to taste, turmeric and salt. Blend in 1 tablespoon ground peanuts and about 2 teaspoons each oil and water to make a thin paste. Rub paste over chicken pieces and leave aside for 1 hour.

Heat remaining oil in a deep pan and lightly brown chicken on all sides, taking care not to burn them. Remove to a plate and add onion to pan. Fry gently until transparent, then add coconut milk, water and peanuts. Stir well and add lemon rind, cinnamon bark, sugar and soya sauce. Return chicken to pan, cover and simmer gently for 40 minutes, stirring occasionally. Remove cover and let chicken simmer gently for further 15 minutes to complete cooking and reduce sauce. Remove lemon rind and cinnamon bark and stir in lemon juice. Serve on boiled rice with Spiced Peanuts and Coconut for extra heat and spice if desired, and a steamed green vegetable.

Beef and Bean Enchiladas

To make this as they do in Mexico would take considerable time as it requires the preparation of sauces and tortillas. Canned, bottled or packaged taco and enchilada sauces and canned tortillas simplify the task.

Mexican Tomato Chili Sauce may be used instead of the commercial taco sauce (see page 106).

1 medium-sized onion, chopped
¼ cup (2 oz) lard
2 cloves garlic, crushed
750 g (1½ lb) ground beef
1 quantity Frijoles de Olla (page 43)
½ cup (4 fl oz) canned or bottled taco sauce
½ cup coarsely chopped stuffed olives
salt to taste
12 tortillas (see page 106)
¼ cup (2 fl oz) oil
2 cups enchilada sauce or 1 package enchilada sauce made according to directions
2 cups (8 oz) shredded cheddar cheese
fresh coriander sprigs and sliced, stuffed olives
sour cream for serving

In a deep pan gently fry onion in lard until soft. Add ground beef, increase heat and fry, stirring often, until meat begins to brown. Prepare beans as directed but do not mash the cup of beans. Instead drain liquid and reserve. Mash beans with potato masher and add to beef with taco sauce and olives. Add salt to taste and enough bean liquid to make mixture moist but not too runny. Bring to the boil and remove from heat.

Fry tortillas one at a time in hot oil in a frying pan. Cook for a few seconds only on each side. Remove and drain on paper towels. Stack them as they are cooked and cover with a cloth to keep warm. Fill tortillas with beef and bean mixture and roll up. Place in a single layer in an oven dish, seam side down and pour enchilada sauce over them. Sprinkle with cheese and bake in a moderate oven for 20 minutes until cheese melts and browns slightly. Garnish with fresh coriander sprigs and sliced stuffed olives and serve with sour cream in a separate bowl, to be added to individual taste.

Chicken and Lentil Casserole

Serves: 6
Oven temperature: 160°C (325°F)

1.5 kg (3 lb) chicken pieces
salt
freshly ground black pepper
125 g (4 oz) streaky bacon, diced
1 tablespoon oil
1 large onion, chopped
1 clove garlic, crushed
1 medium-sized carrot, diced
2 tablespoons tomato paste
½ teaspoon sugar
1 teaspoon white vinegar
1 bay leaf
1 small onion studded with 3 cloves
1 cup (8 oz) split red lentils
2 cups (1 imperial pint) chicken stock

Dry chicken pieces and rub with salt and pepper. Leave aside. Heat a heavy frying pan, add bacon and cook until fat renders and bacon is browned. Remove bacon to a casserole dish, leaving fat in pan. Add oil to fat and brown chicken pieces on all sides. Remove to a plate. To fat left in pan add onion and cook gently until transparent. Add garlic and carrot, cook 1 minute, then add tomato paste, sugar and ½ cup of the chicken stock. Stir well to lift sediment and remove from heat.

Pick over lentils and wash well. Drain and place lentils in casserole dish with the bacon. Add frying pan contents, bay leaf and clove-studded onion. Place chicken pieces on top and pour in remaining stock. Cover casserole tightly and cook in a moderately slow oven for 1¼ hours, or until chicken is tender. Remove bay leaf and onion and discard. Serve casserole with a steamed green vegetable or a tossed side salad.

Persian Lamb and Bean Stew

Serves: 6

1 cup (8 oz) saluggia or red kidney beans
3 cups (1½ imperial pints) water
1 kg (2 lb) lamb stew meat
1 large onion, finely chopped
¼ cup (2 oz) ghee or butter
1 teaspoon turmeric
½ cup (4 fl oz) tomato purée
1 tablespoon lemon juice
salt
freshly ground black pepper

Wash beans well and place in a pan with the water. Bring to the boil, boil 2 minutes. Cover and leave off the heat for 1 hour until plump. Trim lamb and cut into 2 cm (¾ inch) cubes. Heat half the ghee in a deep heavy pan and brown meat on all sides. Remove to a plate. Add remaining ghee to pan and gently fry onion until transparent. Stir in turmeric and cook 2 minutes. Return lamb to pan with plumped beans and their soaking liquid. Add another 2 cups water and bring to the boil. Cover pan and simmer over low heat for 1 hour. Add tomato purée and lemon juice.

Season with salt and pepper to taste and cook further hour or until meat and beans are tender. Serve in deep plates. Pickles, chopped onion, radishes and Arab flat bread should be served as accompaniments.

White Bean Stew

Serves: 6-8

A popular vegetable stew in Greece, Cyprus and Turkey. Any white beans or black-eyed beans may be used – even soya beans are much improved cooked this way but they would have to be boiled for 3 hours in twice the amount of water before adding any other ingredients. Don't forget to drain the soya bean soaking water and add fresh water for boiling. For other beans cook in the soaking water unless you prefer not to.

2 cups (1 lb) dried haricot (navy) beans or other white beans
6 cups water
2 large onions, chopped
½ cup olive oil
2 cloves garlic, chopped
1 large carrot, diced
1 celery stalk (including leaves), chopped
500 g (1 lb) ripe tomatoes, peeled and chopped
1 tablespoon tomato paste
¼ teaspoon sugar
freshly ground black pepper
salt
¼ cup chopped parsley

Wash beans well and place in a large pan. Cover with 6 cups cold water and bring to the boil. Boil for 2 minutes, remove from heat, cover and leave for 1-2 hours until beans are plump. In a frying pan heat oil and sauté onion until transparent. Add garlic, carrot and celery and fry for 5 minutes, stirring often. Set aside. Return beans to the boil and boil gently, covered, for 30 minutes (for 3 hours if using soya beans).

Add fried vegetables, tomatoes, tomato paste, sugar and pepper to taste, cover and simmer for 1¼ hours or until beans are tender without being broken. Add salt to taste and half of the parsley. Cook for 10 minutes longer. Serve in a deep dish sprinkled with remaining parsley. May be served hot or cold.

USING CANNED BEANS: Fry vegetables in oil in a large pan. Add 2 cups water and tomatoes, tomato paste, sugar, salt and pepper. Cover and simmer 30 minutes. Add 3 300 g (10 oz) or 2 440 g (1 lb) cans soya or other white beans with their liquid. Stir in parsley, cover and simmer 15 minutes. This quantity serves 4-5.

Satays with Peanut Sauce

Serves: 6

500 g (1 lb) lean pork loin or tender beef such as sirloin or rump
1 large onion, grated
½ teaspoon finely grated lemon rind
1 clove garlic, crushed
2 tablespoons oil
4 teaspoons soya sauce
2 teaspoons brown sugar
1½ teaspoons ground coriander
1 teaspoon ground cummin
1 teaspoon ground turmeric
⅛-¼ teaspoon chili powder
1 teaspoon salt
1 tablespoon smooth peanut butter
For serving:
Peanut Sauce (page 103)
boiled rice

Meat quantity given is for trimmed, boneless meat, so purchase more than this if cut chosen has fat and bone. Trim and cut into 2 cm (¾ inch) cubes. Soak 6 bamboo skewers in cold water for several hours to prevent them scorching when satays are cooked.

Grate onion into a sieve set over a bowl. Press pulp with the back of a spoon to extract juice and discard pulp. Stir remaining ingredients into onion juice, add meat cubes and toss to coat. Cover and marinate in refrigerator for 2 hours or longer, turning meat occasionally. Thread meat onto skewers with pieces barely touching and coming only halfway up skewers. Cook over glowing coals or under a very hot grill just until meat is cooked to taste – do not overcook. Turn frequently during cooking, brushing with any remaining marinade. Serve with Peanut Sauce, boiled rice and a salad, preferably one including beans.

Bean and Frankfurter Bake

Serves: 6
Oven temperature: 180°C (350°F)

A convenient recipe using canned baked beans in tomato sauce; left-over Boston Baked Beans or Baked Beans in Tomato Sauce may be used instead of the canned beans – *see index for recipes.*

500 g (1 lb) thin frankfurters
2 tablespoons lard or oil
1 large onion, chopped
1 small sweet green pepper, chopped
2 440 g (1 lb) cans baked beans in tomato sauce
salt
freshly ground black pepper

Cut frankfurters diagonally into 5 cm (2 inch) lengths. Grease a frying pan with a little of the lard or oil and fry frankfurter pieces until lightly browned. Remove to a casserole dish.

Add remaining lard or oil to pan with onion and pepper and fry gently until onion is soft. Add to casserole with the baked beans, stir to blend, cover and bake in a moderate oven for 25–30 minutes until heated through. Serve hot from casserole.

Beef and Bean Sprouts

Serves: 4–5

500 g (1 lb) round steak
1 egg white
1 tablespoon cornflour
½ teaspoon bicarbonate of soda
2 tablespoons water
½ teaspoon white vinegar
6 spring onions (scallions)
2 cups (8 oz) bean sprouts
2 tablespoons peanut oil
1 cm (½ inch) piece fresh ginger, bruised
1 clove garlic, bruised
2 tablespoons soya sauce
1 tablespoon dry sherry
2 teaspoons sugar
¼ cup (2 fl oz) water
boiled rice for serving

Trim meat and pound lightly. Cut into thin strips about 5cm (2 inches) long. Place in a bowl and add lightly beaten egg white, cornflour, soda and water. Blend thoroughly until water is absorbed, then stir in vinegar. Cover and leave aside for 30 minutes.

Cut spring onions diagonally into short sections, including some green tops. Pick over bean sprouts, nipping off any browned ends and removing loose skins. Rinse in cold water and drain.

Heat oil in a wok and add bruised ginger and garlic. Cook until browned, remove ginger and garlic and discard. Add meat to flavoured oil and stir-fry over high heat until browned and cooked through. Add spring onions and stir-fry 1 minute, then add bean sprouts. Toss well and remove wok from heat. Blend soya sauce with sherry, sugar and water. Return wok to heat and pour in soya sauce mixture. Stir over heat until boiling and serve immediately with boiled rice.

Chili Corn-Pone Pie

Serves: 5–6
Oven temperature: 200°C (400°F)

Use the blended chili powder for the beef and bean mixture — that is the one which contains ground hot chili, dried oregano and cummin.

1 tablespoon oil
1 large onion, chopped
1 clove garlic, crushed
500 g (1 lb) ground beef
1 440 g (1 lb) can peeled tomatoes, chopped
3 teaspoons blended chili powder
¼ cup tomato catsup or sauce
½ cup chopped sweet green pepper
salt
freshly ground black pepper
1 440 g (1 lb) can red kidney beans or 2 cups cooked red kidney beans

Corn-pone Crust:
1 cup (6 oz) yellow corn meal
½ cup (2 oz) plain flour
2 teaspoons baking powder
¼ teaspoon salt
1 teaspoon sugar
1 egg, beaten
½ cup (4 fl oz) milk
¼ cup (2 oz) butter, melted

Heat oil in a pan and add onion. Fry gently until transparent. Add garlic, cook a few seconds then add ground beef. Increase heat and cook, stirring often to break up lumps. When meat begins to brown reduce heat and add tomatoes, blended chili powder, tomato catsup or sauce, chopped pepper and salt and pepper to taste. Cover and simmer for 20 minutes. Add drained beans, cover and cook for further 10 minutes. Turn into a 6-cup casserole or deep pie dish and keep hot.

Sift cornmeal with flour, baking powder and salt into a bowl. Stir in sugar. Beat egg into milk and pour into dry ingredients with the melted butter. Mix to a smooth, thick batter. Carefully place spoonfuls of batter evenly over hot chili mixture then spread batter out with a spatula to edges of dish. Bake in a hot oven for 20 minutes. Serve hot.

Moroccan Chicken and Chick Peas

Serves: 5-6

1 cup (8 oz) chick peas, soaked (page 9)
4 cups (2 imperial pints) water
1.5 kg (3 lb) chicken pieces
1 teaspoon turmeric
½ teaspoon ground cummin
salt
⅛ teaspoon cayenne pepper
2 tablespoons oil
1 large onion, finely chopped
juice of 1 lemon
lemon wedges to garnish

Wash and soak chick peas in the water, using either the slow or quick soak methods. Put into a deep pan and bring to the boil, skimming when necessary. Cover and boil gently for 1½ hours.

Dry chicken pieces with paper towels. Combine turmeric and cummin with 1 teaspoon salt and the cayenne pepper and rub into chicken. Let stand for 15 minutes. Heat oil in a frying pan and brown chicken pieces on all sides. Remove to a plate and add onion to pan. Fry gently until soft, add garlic and cook a few seconds. Pour onion mixture into partly cooked chick peas and add chicken pieces and 1 tablespoon of the lemon juice. Cover and simmer gently for further hour or until chicken and chick peas are tender and liquid is considerably reduced. Taste and add salt if necessary, and more lemon juice to give a pleasant tang. Remove chicken pieces carefully, place chick peas and liquid in a deep dish, put the chicken pieces on top and garnish with lemon wedges.

Brazilian Bean Pot

FEIJOADA

Serves: 12–15

The Feijoada of Brazil is another of those hearty bean dishes designed to feed a multitude. To scale down the recipe for a family meal is impossible as the essential character of the dish would be lost. In Brazil it is a favoured Sunday lunch served in restaurants; I suggest you serve it to guests as an al-fresco lunch on a sunny weekend or holiday – and after this feast, a siesta would be mandatory.

4 cups (2 lb) Mexican black beans, soaked (page 9)
12 cups (6 imperial pints) water
1 smoked ox tongue (uncooked)
1.5 kg (3 lb) corned brisket beef
1 kg (2 lb) chuck in one piece
250 g (8 oz) bacon or salt pork in one piece
500 g (1 lb) smoked chorizo sausages
1 tablespoon lard
1 large onion, finely chopped
2 cloves garlic, finely chopped
¼–½ teaspoon tabasco sauce
For serving:
boiled rice
peeled orange slices or segments
Vinegared Onions (see end of method)

Pick over beans and soak overnight using the slow salt soak. Drain, rinse well and place in a large pot. Add fresh water to just cover beans and bring to the boil. Cover pot and boil beans gently for 1 hour.

Rinse tongue and brisket, place in a separate pot with water to cover. Bring to a slow simmer, cover and simmer for 1 hour. Add chuck and bacon or salt pork, return to the boil and skim well before liquid boils. Cover and boil gently for 15 minutes. Put meats in with partly cooked beans and add enough of the strained meat stock to cover pot contents. Bring to a slow simmer, cover and cook for 1 hour. Add chorizo sausages and cook until beans and meats are tender, adding more meat stock as required.

Lift out tongue, leave until cool enough to handle and pull off skin. Remove gristle and bone from base of tongue. Place on a large platter with the other meats and the sausages. Cover and keep warm.

Heat lard in a frying pan, add onion and fry gently until soft. Add garlic and cook a few seconds longer. Ladle 2 cups cooked beans into the pan and mash well with the onions and garlic. Add tabasco sauce to taste and turn mashed beans into the bean pot. Stir well, adjust seasoning with salt and tabasco sauce if necessary. Pour beans into a chafing dish, cover and place on table.

Slice the meats, arranging them in groups on the platter, or carve meats at the table. Serve boiled rice, prepared oranges and Vinegared Onions separately. Traditionally a bowl of shredded kale or collard greens is also served; the leaves are shredded and cooked in a little lard with a little chopped onion until the vegetable wilts, then covered and simmered for 15 minutes. Broccoli florets may be substituted if kale or collard is unavailable.

Vinegared Onions: Thinly slice 2 large Spanish onions into a bowl and sprinkle with salt to taste. Add ¼ cup each brown vinegar and salad oil. Stir well and leave aside for 30 minutes. If Spanish onions are not available, use white onions. These must be sliced and covered with boiling water. Drain, rinse in cold water and drain again. Add salt, vinegar and oil as above.

Hungarian Pork and Beans

Serves: 6-8

A Hungarian way to extend pork for a satisfying meal. Smoked uncooked pork is the usual meat required; gammon, lean bacon, smoked ham butt or the Spanish smoked ham called laçon may be used. The amount given is for the boneless meat; if bone is included in your purchase, buy about 125 g (4 oz) more to allow for loss when trimming.

2 cups (8 oz) cannellini, Great Northern or haricot (navy) beans
6 cups (3 imperial pints) water
2 tablespoons lard
1 large onion, finely chopped
1 clove garlic, crushed
1 fresh red chili, seeded and chopped
2 chicken stock cubes
4 teaspoons paprika
500 g (1 lb) smoked pork (see above for substitutions)
salt to taste

Wash beans well, place in a pan with water and bring to the boil. Boil 2 minutes, remove from heat, cover and leave for 1 hour until beans are plump. Return to the boil and cook gently for 30 minutes. Trim pork, removing any skin or bone, and cut into 1 cm (½ inch) cubes.

In a heavy pan heat lard and add onion. Fry gently until transparent and lightly browned. Add meat cubes, garlic and chopped chili and cook for 10 minutes, stirring often. Pour in about 2 cups bean liquid, crumble in stock cubes and add paprika. Bring to the boil. Drain remaining liquid from beans and reserve. Put beans into pan, adding a little more liquid if necessary so that contents are just covered with liquid. Cover and cook on low heat for 1 hour until beans are tender, removing lid for last 15 minutes of cooking so that sauce thickens, increasing heat if necessary. Add salt to taste when lid is removed. Serve with rye or black bread.

Note: If you have difficulty in purchasing suitable smoked pork in your area, use 500 g (1 lb) lean boneless fresh pork and add 125 g (4 oz) cracked bacon bones to give a smoky flavour.

Chili Beef and Bean Casserole

Serves: 6

Oven temperature: 160°C (325°F)

1½ cups (12 oz) cannellini or Great Northern beans
5 cups (2½ imperial pints) water
750 g (1½ lb) chuck steak
2 tablespoons oil
1 large onion, chopped
2 cloves garlic, crushed
1 cup chopped, peeled tomatoes
2 tablespoons tomato paste
2 cups (1 imperial pint) stock
3 teaspoons blended chili powder
½ teaspoon sugar
salt to taste
1 small sweet green pepper

Wash and quick soak beans according to directions on page 9, using given quantity of water. When plump return to the boil, cover and simmer gently for 1-1½ hours or until almost tender. Drain and keep aside.

Cut beef into 2 cm (¾ inch) cubes. Heat oil in a pan and brown beef on all sides, transferring to a casserole dish when browned. Add onion to pan, fry gently until soft and stir in garlic, then tomatoes, tomato paste, stock, chili powder, sugar and about 2 teaspoons salt. Add beans, stir and cover casserole tightly. Cook in a moderately slow oven for 1½ hours. Seed pepper and chop roughly. Add to casserole and cook for further 30 minutes, adding a little more stock if necessary. Serve hot from casserole.

Note: Blended chili powder is a combination of hot chili powder, ground coriander, cummin etc., a combination often used for Chili Con Carne. Do not use pure chili powder or pepper in this recipe in above quantity.

Lamb, Chick Pea and Lentil Stew

DHANSAK

Serves: 6–8

This Parsi dish from India is just right for entertaining, particularly if your family and friends have exotic tastes. Chicken may be used in place of the lamb, and you would require 2 kg (4 lb) chicken pieces at least, taking bones into account.

½ cup (4 oz) chick peas
1 cup (8 oz) yellow split peas
½ cup (4 oz) mung beans
½ cup (4 oz) split red lentils
water
1.5 kg (3 lb) boneless lamb
3 large onions
1 medium-sized eggplant
salt
1 large potato
250 g (8 oz) butternut or other pumpkin
250 g (8 oz) spinach
¼ cup ghee or butter
4 cloves garlic, crushed
2–6 fresh chilis, seeded and finely chopped
2 teaspoons grated fresh ginger
¼ cup chopped coriander leaves
¼ cup chopped mint leaves
2 teaspoons ground turmeric
2 teaspoons ground cummin
2 teaspoons garam masala
½ teaspoon freshly ground pepper
For serving:
lemon wedges
boiled rice
Onion Sambal (page 100)
Chapatis (page 98)

Wash chick peas, place in a large pan and add 3 cups water. Bring to the boil, boil 2 minutes and remove from heat. Cover and leave aside for 1–2 hours until plump. Meanwhile prepare remaining ingredients. Pick over other pulses, put them all in a sieve and wash well. Drain and leave aside. Trim lamb and cut into large cubes. Peel onions, chop one and put aside. Halve remaining onions lengthwise and slice into semicircles. Dice eggplant and sprinkle generously with salt. Leave in a colander. Peel potato and pumpkin and cut into large pieces. Remove roots from spinach and discard, wash leaves and stalks well and chop roughly. Prepare remaining ingredients, using maximum amount of chilis if a very hot flavour is preferred.

When chick peas are plump, bring to the boil, cover and boil gently for 1½ hours. Add another 3 cups water and the other washed pulses. Return to the boil, uncovered.

Meanwhile heat 1 tablespoon ghee in a large frying pan and add the lamb cubes. Stir over high heat until meat loses red colour and tip meat and ghee into chick peas etc. Add chopped onion, potato, pumpkin, rinsed eggplant, spinach and 2 teaspoons salt. When boiling gently, reduce heat, cover pan and simmer gently for 1½ hours or until meat and chick peas are tender. Other ingredients would be cooked in this time. Do not stir during cooking, that way ingredients will not catch. However it may be necessary to add a little more water if contents look dry.

Remove meat pieces to a plate. Mash remaining ingredients in pan with potato masher, or purée in batches in food processor and turn into a bowl.

Melt remaining ghee in a large, heavy pan and fry the sliced onions until golden brown. Remove half of these to a plate. Add garlic, chopped chilis, herbs, ginger and spices to pan and stir over heat for 2–3 minutes. Add meat pieces, stir well, then stir in puréed pulse-vegetable mixture. Adjust seasoning, cover and simmer gently for 15 minutes. Transfer to a deep serving dish and garnish with reserved browned onion, lemon wedges and herb sprigs. Serve with boiled rice, Onion Sambal and Chapatis.

Herbed Lamb with Flageolets

Serves: 4–6

Oven temperature: 190° C (375° F)

Flageolets are rarely available outside Western Europe in dried form. Canned flageolets are usually available in gourmet food stores. While haricot or navy beans may be substituted, I prefer to substitute baby green lima beans for their colour and better flavour.

1½ cups (12 oz) flageolets or baby lima beans
4 cups (2 imperial pints) water
1 carrot, quartered
1 onion studded with 3 cloves
bouquet garni
salt
1 loin lamb, about 1.5 kg (3 lb)
2 cloves garlic, crushed
freshly ground black pepper
3 sprigs fresh rosemary
2 sprigs fresh thyme
2 bay leaves
2 tablespoon melted butter
½ cup (4 fl oz) dry white wine
½ cup (4 fl oz) bean liquid
3 teaspoons flour
To finish:
¼ cup (2 oz) butter
¼ cup (2 fl oz) cream
1 tablespoon chopped parsley

Wash and quick-soak beans according to directions on page 9. When plump return to heat and add carrot, clove-studded onion and bouquet garni. Return to the boil and boil gently, covered, for 1 hour, adding salt to taste after 45 minutes.

Meanwhile prepare lamb. Saw through chine bone in 6–8 places, or have meat supplier do this when purchasing. Alternatively chine and rib bones can be removed altogether. Remove fine skin from fat surface of loin. Open out loin and place fat side down on board. Rub inner surface with 1 crushed clove garlic and season with salt and pepper. Put 2 of the rosemary sprigs, the thyme sprigs and bay leaves along the length of the loin and sprinkle with melted butter. Roll up and tie securely with white string. Rub fat with remaining garlic, salt and pepper. Strip leaves off remaining rosemary sprig and press onto fat. Place loin on a rack in roasting pan and roast in a moderately hot oven for 50 minutes. Remove lamb to a hot dish, take off string, unroll and remove herbs. Reroll and leave in a warm place.

Skim most of fat from pan juices and stir in flour. Place over heat and cook 2 minutes. Pour in wine and liquid from beans, stirring occasionally. When thickened and bubbling, adjust seasoning and strain into a gravy boat.

Drain cooked beans and remove carrot, bouquet garni and onion. Add the butter and cream and toss over heat for a minute or two. Put into a vegetable dish and sprinkle with chopped parsley. Carve lamb into chops or thick slices and serve with the gravy and the beans.

Note: If using canned flageolets, use 2 cans (each about 440g or 1 pound) and heat them in their liquid. When boiling, drain well and return to the pan with butter and cream. Serve as above.

LIGHT BEANFEASTS

While beans may be considered as a robust food, there are many ways to prepare them for light luncheons and suppers. Cabbage Rolls with Chick Peas and Rice are a pleasant change from the traditional meat-filled rolls; a spicy bowl of Dhal is pure delight; deliciously light Chinese Bean Sprout Omelets; a simple dish of Black-eyed Beans and Silverbeet. Try them once, and you will try them again.

Spiced Black Gram Purée

Serves: 6

1 cup (8 oz) black gram (urad)
4 cups (2 imperial pints) water
salt
1 dried red chili
2 tablespoons ghee or butter
1 medium-sized onion, finely chopped
2 cloves garlic, finely chopped
½ teaspoon ground turmeric
½ teaspoon finely chopped fresh ginger
¼ teaspoon garam masala
For serving:
boiled rice
Chapatis (page 98)

Pick over black gram and wash well in several changes of water. Place in a heavy pan and add water. Bring slowly to the boil, and boil gently on low heat for 45 minutes until very soft and broken apart.

Halve chili and remove seeds and membrane. Chop roughly. Heat ghee or butter in a frying pan on low heat and add onion and garlic. Fry gently until onion is soft. Add turmeric, ginger and chili, increase heat and fry for further 5 minutes until onion begins to brown. Pour into simmering black gram and stir in garam masala. Simmer, uncovered, for 10 minutes and serve with boiled rice and Chapatis.

Popular Indian ingredients and pulse dishes — top shelf from left — tamarind, split red lentils, yellow split peas; below right — mung beans husked and whole; left — black gram husked and whole, and Dhal, page 68. Foreground — Lentil and Rice Pancakes, page 75.

Chinese Bean Sprout Omelets

Serves: 6

1½ cups (6 oz) bean sprouts
6 spring onions (scallions)
6 eggs
salt to taste
peanut oil for frying
Sauce:
1 cup (8 fl oz) cold chicken stock
1 teaspoon sugar
3 teaspoons cornflour
2 teaspoons soy sauce
2 thin slices fresh ginger root
salt to taste

Rinse bean sprouts thoroughly in cold water. Nip off any browned tips and remove loose skins. Drain thoroughly. Clean spring onions leaving most of green tops. Thinly slice some of the green tops diagonally and put aside for garnish; chop remaining onions finely. Beat eggs with salt to taste. When slightly frothy stir in bean sprouts and chopped spring onions. Blend sauce ingredients in a small pan and heat, stirring constantly until bubbling. Leave on low heat to simmer gently.

Heat 2 teaspoons oil in a frying pan or wok and pour in ½ cup of the egg mixture. Cook until browned on the bottom, turn and cook other side. Remove to a plate set over gently simmering water. Repeat until all egg mixture is cooked, adding more oil to pan or wok as required. Stack 2 or 3 omelets on each plate, pour over some of the sauce and garnish with reserved spring onion tops.

Variations: Add about 1 cup finely chopped cooked chicken or prawns to eggs with the other ingredients.

Honey-Soya Chicken Wings

Serves: 6

1.5 kg (3 lb) chicken wings
¼ cup (2 fl oz) soya sauce
¼ cup (2 fl oz) lemon juice
¼ cup (2 fl oz) honey
1 teaspoon grated fresh ginger
1 clove garlic, crushed
2 tablespoons peanut oil

Cut off wing tips and keep for stock. Wipe chicken wings dry with paper towels. Combine remaining ingredients in a glass bowl and add chicken wings. Turn to coat, cover and marinate in refrigerator for 2 hours or longer. Turn wings occasionally.

Lift wings from marinade and place on rack in griller (broiler) pan. Cook under pre-heated griller for 15–20 minutes, with chicken 8 cm (3 inches) from heat source. Care must be taken that wings cook through without burning. Brush with marinade and turn frequently during cooking. When golden brown and crisp on the outside, remove to a warm platter and serve. Good as a light lunch with Stir-fried Bean Sprouts (page 91), or serve as a finger food with drinks.

To cook on barbecue: Place on barbecue grid over glowing coals, lifting grid high to begin with so that wings can cook slowly. Lower towards end of cooking to crisp them. Brush frequently with marinade.

Cabbage Rolls, page 78, and Chick Pea and Eggplant Stew, page 87.

Dhal

Serves: 4

1 cup (8 oz) split red lentils
2½ cups (1¼ imperial pints) water
2 medium-sized onions
2 tablespoons ghee or oil
2 cloves garlic, finely chopped
½ teaspoon grated fresh ginger
½ teaspoon turmeric
½ teaspoon cummin
¼ teaspoon ground coriander
1 fresh red chili, seeded and chopped
juice of ½ lemon
chopped fresh coriander, optional
For serving:
boiled rice
Chapatis (page 98)

Wash lentils well, place in a pan and add cold water. Bring to the boil, skimming when necessary. Chop 1 onion finely and add to lentils. Cover and simmer gently for 30 minutes until soft. Do not stir once lentils begin to boil.

Halve remaining onion lengthwise then slice into semi-circles. Heat ghee or oil and fry onion until well flecked with brown. Remove half of the onion and keep aside. Add garlic, ginger, turmeric, cummin, coriander and chili to onion in pan and fry on medium heat for 2 minutes, stirring constantly. Add to lentils with salt to taste, stir gently and simmer with lid off pan until purée is the consistency of thin porridge. Pour into a bowl and garnish with reserved browned onion and chopped coriander if desired. Serve with boiled rice and Chapatis.

Note: Yellow split peas or other lentils may be used in place of the red lentils. Cooking times may need to be lengthened.

Dhal with Cabbage

Serves: 5–6

Freshly grated coconut is preferable for this Indian dish. However desiccated coconut moistened with water (¼ cup water to 1 cup coconut) is a reasonable substitute.

1 cup (8 oz) yellow split peas
2 cups (1 imperial pint) water
2 medium sized onions
2 green chilis, seeded
½ small head cabbage
salt
2 tablespoons ghee or butter
2 curry leaves
1 teaspoon black mustard seeds
1 teaspoon husked black gram
½ teaspoon ground turmeric
½ cup (2 oz) freshly grated coconut
For serving:
boiled rice
Onion Sambal (page 100)
Chapatis (page 98)

Pick over split peas, wash well and place in a large pan with the water. Bring to the boil and skim well. When boiling reduce heat, put 1 chopped onion and 1 chopped chili on top of split peas and cover pan. Simmer gently for 45 minutes or until split peas are tender. Do not stir.

Shred cabbage finely, place on top of dhal, add about 1½ teaspoons salt and cover pan. Leave on medium low heat for 10 minutes or until cabbage is soft.

Meanwhile slice remaining onion and lightly brown in ghee in a frying pan. Add second finely chopped chili, curry leaves, mustard seeds, husked black gram and turmeric. Fry on medium heat until mustard seeds begin popping. Remove from heat. When cabbage is tender, pour frying pan contents over cabbage, add coconut and stir into split peas. Serve with boiled rice, Onion Sambal and Chapatis.

Black-Eyed Beans with Silverbeet

Serves: 6

2 cups (1 lb) black-eyed beans
6 cups (3 imperial pints) water
salt
1 kg (2 lb) silverbeet (Swiss chard)
2 cloves garlic, optional
½ cup olive oil
juice of 1 lemon
lemon wedges for serving

Wash dried beans well, place in a pan and cover with the 6 cups water. Bring to the boil, boil uncovered for 2 minutes and remove from heat. Cover pan and leave for 1 hour or until plump. Bring to a slow simmer, cover and simmer gently for 1½ hours or until just tender.

Wash silverbeet in several changes of water. Cut off stalks and trim them. Cut stalks in 1 cm (½ inch) pieces and add to beans with salt to taste. Cover and cook for further 10 minutes. Shred silverbeet leaves coarsely and add to beans. Cover and cook for further 15 minutes or until beans and silverbeet are tender. Drain well and turn into a deep bowl. Crush garlic with a little salt if used. Blend into olive oil with lemon juice and pour over hot vegetables. Toss well and serve with lemon wedges so that flavour may be adjusted to individual taste. Serve hot or warm.

Thunder and Lightning

Which is the thunder and which is the lightning is a matter for conjecture, as this Italian dish is a mixture of pasta and chick peas. The pasta usually consists of broken bits and pieces of various types sold cheaply in Italian food stores (in Italy – not where pasta comes in neat plastic packages). The nutty, crunchy taste and texture of the chick peas is a pleasant contrast to the pasta, cooked *al dente* of course.

1 cup (8 oz) chick peas, soaked (see page 9)
water
salt
1 cup (6 oz) mixed pasta pieces or use one type only
¼ cup (2 fl oz) olive oil
1 clove garlic, crushed, optional
2 tablespoons chopped parsley
grated Parmesan cheese

Slow or quick soak chick peas, drain and place in a pan with about 4 cups water. Bring to the boil and boil gently, covered, for 2½-3 hours until tender, adding salt to taste towards end of cooking. After cooking most of liquid should be absorbed, otherwise boil uncovered until about ½ cup remains.

Boil pasta in salted water until just tender to the bite *(al dente)*. Drain and mix into cooked chick peas. Heat olive oil in a pan, add garlic, cook a few seconds and remove from heat. Stir in parsley and pour into peas and pasta. Add about 2 tablespoons Parmesan cheese, toss well and serve in a deep dish with extra cheese in a separate bowl. Variations: Fry some diced bacon and add to peas and pasta with the olive oil and garlic mixture.

Make as above and serve with a tomato spaghetti sauce.

Hot Beans,Vegetables Provençal

Serves: 6

A delicious combination from Provence, ideal for outdoor eating. Use canned beans for convenience, or cook dried beans from scratch, but you will have to cook them separately as times vary and flavours mingle. However if you do a bit of bean cooking, stock-pile 1½ cups of each of 3 varieties in the refrigerator. Store in their cooking liquid in sealed containers — they will keep a week providing salt has been added during last stages of cooking.

3 small beetroot (beets)
250 g (8 oz) young green beans
250 g (8 oz) baby carrots, scraped
1½ cups cooked chick peas
1½ cups cooked haricot (navy) or cannellini beans
1½ cups cooked saluggia or red kidney beans
1 x 425 g (1 lb) can globe artichoke hearts
6-12 hard boiled eggs
1 quantity Aioli (page 104)

Scrub beetroot and cook in boiling, salted water until tender. Peel and keep warm. Top and tail beans, string only if necessary and leave whole. Cook with the carrots in boiling salted water for 5 minutes until just tender, drain in a sieve, run cold water over them, place in a deep, oval dish and keep warm.

Combine cooked chick peas and beans and the liquid from the lighter coloured beans and reheat in a pan until boiling. Drain and add to green beans and carrots in dish. Heat globe artichokes in a pan, drain, cut in half and add to dish. Toss vegetables lightly together. Cut beetroot into quarters and arrange around edge of dish. Pile just-cooked hard-boiled eggs in another dish, still in their shells.

Serve Aioli in a bowl. Each diner takes a portion of vegetables and blends in Aioli to taste. Eggs are shelled and dipped into Aioli by each person. Serve with plenty of crusty bread and a chilled white wine for a complete meal.

Note: Of course in Provence they would not dream of using canned artichokes, but with all the other preparation involved, the canned vegetable is a time saver. Alternatively prepare and cook 6 globe artichokes, trimmed to the heart (inner leaves), drain well, halve and remove chokes.

Lentil and Corn Patties

Serves: 6

1½ cups (12 oz) split red lentils
3 cups (1½ imperial pints) water
1 onion, finely chopped
1 cup cooked corn kernels, drained
1 egg, beaten
2 tablespoons finely chopped sweet green pepper
2 teaspoons salt
freshly ground black pepper
To finish:
flour for coating
1 egg
2 tablespoons milk
dried breadcrumbs
oil for shallow frying

Pick over lentils and wash well. Put in a heavy pan with the water and bring to the boil. Skim thoroughly, cover and cook on low heat for 45 minutes without stirring. When soft tilt pan, and if water is still present, leave uncovered on medium low heat to evaporate moisture. Stir to a purée; mixture is thick enough when it holds its shape. Turn purée into a bowl and leave until cool.

Blend onion into lentils with corn, egg, green pepper, salt and pepper to taste. Chill for 1-2 hours to firm mixture. Stir in 1-2 tablespoons breadcrumbs if mixture is too soft. Shape generous tablespoons of mixture into thick patties 4 cm (1½ inches) in diameter. Coat with flour, egg beaten with milk, then breadcrumbs. Shallow fry in hot oil for 3 minutes each side until golden brown. Drain on paper towels and serve hot with vegetable accompaniment or salad.

Mung Beans with Yoghurt

Serves: 6

1 cup (8 oz) mung beans
3 cups (1½ imperial pints) water
1 clove garlic
⅛ teaspoon ground coriander
⅛ teaspoon ground cummin
½ teaspoon chili powder
½ teaspoon ground turmeric
1 cup (8 fl oz) plain yoghurt
additional water
salt to taste
2 tablespoons chopped fresh coriander
boiled rice for serving

Pick over mung beans and wash well. Place in a heavy pan with the water and bring slowly to the boil. Cover and boil gently for 45 minutes until soft. Remove from heat and leave aside, covered, for 15 minutes. Meanwhile crush garlic to a paste and blend in coriander, cummin, chili powder and turmeric. Put yoghurt in a bowl and stir in an equal amount of cold water. Blend until smooth and stir in the garlic mixture. Pour this into the cooked mung beans and return to heat. Add salt to taste and cook, uncovered, on low heat for 30 minutes, stirring often. Take care that mixture does not catch on base of pan. Serve hot over boiled rice, sprinkled with chopped coriander.

Split Pea and Potato Curry

Serves: 4-5

1 cup (8 oz) yellow split peas
2 cups (1 imperial pint) water
500 g (1 lb) potatoes
2 tablespoons ghee or oil
1 large onion, finely chopped
1 teaspoon grated fresh ginger
2 cloves garlic, crushed
1 teaspoon turmeric
¼-½ teaspoon chili powder
salt to taste
½ teaspoon garam masala or ground allspice
1 tablespoon chopped fresh coriander leaves
1 tablespoon lemon juice
For serving:
additional chopped fresh coriander
lemon wedges

Wash split peas well, place in a pan with water and bring to the boil, skimming when necessary. Cover and boil gently on low heat for 45 minutes or until very soft with little moisture left. Scrub potatoes and boil in jackets until tender. Drain, peel and dice. In a frying pan heat ghee or oil and add onion. Fry until lightly browned, add ginger and garlic, turmeric and chili powder to taste and fry for 2 minutes. Stir in split peas and potatoes. Add salt to taste, garam masala or allspice, fresh coriander and lemon juice. Cover and leave on low heat for 10 minutes, adding a little water if too dry. Serve sprinkled with additional chopped coriander and garnish with lemon wedges.

Split Pea Purée

FAVA

Serves: 4-6

A favourite Greek dish, particularly during Lent or other fasting periods. Though it is called fava, yellow split peas are always used. The name fava or faba is given to various beans in different countries, particularly to dried broad beans, Egyptian brown beans (ful) and even white kidney beans.

2 cups (1 lb) yellow split peas
4 cups (2 imperial pints) water
1 onion, chopped
1½ teaspoons salt
olive oil
lemon wedges

Pick over split peas, discarding any that are discoloured. Wash well and place in a heavy-based saucepan. Cover with cold water and bring to the boil. Skim and add chopped onion. Cover and simmer gently without stirring for 2 hours until very soft. Stir in salt and ladle purée into deep plates. Spoon 1-2 tablespoons olive oil onto each serve and accompany with wedges of lemon for squeezing onto purée.

Note: Crusty bread, side dishes of finely sliced onion, black olives and sliced tomato and cucumber in oil and vinegar dressing may also be served with fava.

Spicy Chick Peas

CHOLAY

Serves: 5-6

Spicy and mildly hot, this Indian dish from the Punjab could almost be classed as a dry curry. Serve with Chapatis or even ordinary wholemeal bread, though in the Punjab a fried wholemeal bread called Bhatura is the traditional accompaniment.

1½ cups (12 oz) chick peas
5 cups (2½ imperial pints) water
1 green chili
1 large onion, finely chopped
2 tablespoons ghee or oil
2 cloves garlic, finely chopped
1 teaspoon grated fresh ginger
½ teaspoon ground turmeric
½ teaspoon ground cardamom
½ teaspoon ground cummin
1 teaspoon ground coriander
1 teaspoon garam masala or ground allspice
¼-½ teaspoon chili powder
500 g (1 lb) ripe tomatoes, peeled and chopped
1 tablespoon chopped fresh coriander or mint
salt to taste
fresh coriander or mint sprigs to garnish

Wash chick peas well, put in a pan with water and bring to the boil. Boil 2 minutes, remove from heat, cover and leave aside for 1 hour until plump. Return to the boil, skimming well. Remove stem from chili, cut in half across middle and add to peas. Cover and boil gently for 2 hours or until soft, or cook in pressure cooker for 20 minutes under high pressure. Drain, reserving liquid; remove chili and discard.

In a frying pan fry onion gently in ghee or oil until soft, add garlic, ginger and spices and fry gently for 3 minutes. Stir in tomatoes and chopped herb. Bring to the boil then pour into pan of chick peas. Add salt to taste and about ½ cup reserved liquid, cover and simmer gently for 20 minutes, adding a little more liquid as it is absorbed by the peas. Finished dish should be just moist. Serve hot garnished with fresh herb sprigs and Chapatis or other wholemeal bread.

Bean and Tuna Bake

Serves: 4-6
Oven temperature: 180°C (350°F)

Use canned beans for this one so that you can cook a nourishing lunch quickly. If you want to start from scratch, then cook 1½ cups (12 oz) of the beans specified in their dried form. Follow directions on page 10.

1 quantity White Sauce (page 108)
1 teaspoon French mustard
pinch cayenne pepper
1 cup (4 oz) grated tasty cheddar cheese
2 440g (1 lb) cans white lima or butter beans
1 440 g (1 lb) can tuna (tunny fish) in brine
1 tablespoon lemon juice
1 cup (2 oz) soft breadcrumbs
1 tablespoon melted butter

Make up sauce according to directions and blend in mustard, cayenne and cheese. Stir until smooth and remove from heat.

Drain beans and place half of them in the base of a greased casserole dish. Drain and flake tuna and spread over beans. Sprinkle with lemon juice and pour over half the sauce. Top with remaining beans and spread rest of sauce on top. Toss breadcrumbs in melted butter and sprinkle evenly on top. Bake in a moderate oven for 30 minutes until heated through and top is golden brown. Serve with a steamed green vegetable.

Green Pea Soufflé

Serves: 4
Oven Temperature: 160°C (325°F)

½ cup (4 oz) split green peas
1½ cups (12 fl oz) water
salt to taste
freshly ground black pepper
pinch ground nutmeg
2 spring onions (scallions), chopped, including some tops
4 eggs, separated
butter for greasing
2 teaspoons soft breadcrumbs

Wash split peas well, place in a pan with the water and bring slowly to the boil. Skim well, cover and simmer on low heat for 1-1½ hours until very soft. Remove lid and leave on the heat until excess moisture evaporates. Stir well to a purée – it should be thick enough to form soft peaks. Turn into a bowl and cool – purée will become firmer. Blend in salt and pepper to taste, spring onions and egg yolks. Grease a 5-cup souffle dish with butter and dust with breadcrumbs. Beat egg whites until stiff and fold into pea mixture, using a metal spoon.

Pour into prepared dish and bake in a pre-heated, moderately slow oven for 30-35 minutes. Souffle is cooked when it barely trembles when dish is gently moved. Serve hot with a tossed mixed salad generously moistened with French dressing.

Lentil and Rice Pancakes

DHOSAI

Makes 12-15

These tender Indian pancakes take a little time to prepare, but are a delightful change to the usual pancake. Serve them plain with Rasam or the Indian soup, Sambhar, or with Spiced Potatoes or Spiced Spinach and Lentils.

½ cup (4 oz) husked black gram (urad dhal)
1 cup (8 oz) short grain rice
cold water
1 teaspoon salt
ghee or oil for cooking
For serving:
Rasam (page 21), Spiced Potatotes (page 76) or Spiced Spinach and Lentils (page 76)

Pick over husked black gram to remove any stones or damaged grains. Put into a sieve and wash well under running water. Place in a bowl with 1½ cups water. Wash rice if necessary and place in a separate bowl with 1½ cups water. Leave to soak for 6-8 hours. Drain both black gram and rice, reserving the liquid from each. Put black gram in blender jar and grind, adding enough soaking liquid to draw the gram over the blades (about ⅓ cup). When smooth pour into mixing bowl.

Put rice into jar (no need to rinse it) and add about ½ cup soaking liquid or enough to draw rice over blades. Grind as fine as possible then strain through a fine sieve into the black gram. Stir in salt to taste and if necessary add some of the reserved black gram soaking water to give a thin cream consistency. Cover and leave in a warm place for 3-4 hours – no longer. If making ahead of time, cover and refrigerate after this time.

Heat a pancake pan and grease with a wad of paper towel dipped in ghee or oil. Pour in about ¼ cup batter and tilt pan to spread batter evenly. Cook until browned on base and top is dry, turn and cook other side. Stack and cover to keep warm. Grease pan regularly while cooking. Serve warm with Rasam, as a soup accompaniment, or filled with Spiced Potatoes or Spiced Spinach and Lentils. If served with a filling, Rasam can be served separately to be added to individual taste.

Persian Meatballs and Beans

Serves: 5–6

1½ cups (12 oz) saluggia or cranberry beans
5 cups (2½ imperial pints) water
salt
500 g (1 lb) finely ground beef
1 small onion, grated
¼ cup (1 oz) dried breadcrumbs
1 egg
freshly ground black pepper
¼ teaspoon ground nutmeg
¼ teaspoon ground cinnamon
2 tablespoons oil
1 large onion, sliced
3 tablespoons plum jam
1–2 tablespoons lemon juice
½ teaspoon ground allspice

Wash beans well and quick soak according to directions on page 9 . When plump return to the boil and boil gently, covered, for 1 hour, adding salt to taste after 45 minutes. Beans should be almost tender.

Put ground meat in a bowl with grated onion, crumbs, egg, salt and pepper to taste, nutmeg and cinnamon. Blend lightly and thoroughly and shape into meatballs the size of a small walnut.

Heat oil in a deep pan and brown meatballs on all sides. Remove to a plate. Add sliced onion to pan and fry gently until transparent. Stir in 1½ cups liquid from beans, jam, lemon juice to taste and allspice. Drain beans, reserving any liquid. Add beans to pan, put meatballs on top and cover pan. Simmer gently for 30–45 minutes until beans are tender, adding more liquid if necessary. Serve in deep plates with crusty bread, pickles and a side salad.

Spiced Potatoes

Serves: 4-5

500 g (1 lb) even-sized potatoes
2 tablespoons ghee or oil
1 teaspoon black mustard seeds
1 large onion, finely chopped
½ teaspoon ground turmeric
½ teaspoon chili powder
1 tablespoon chopped fresh coriander leaves
salt to taste
¼ cup water
1 tablespoon lemon juice

Scrub potatoes and boil in their skins in salted water until just tender. Peel and cut into 1 cm (½ inch) dice. In a deep frying pan with lid to fit heat ghee or oil and add mustard seeds. Stir over heat and when they begin to pop, add onion. Fry for 10 minutes, stirring often, until soft and lightly browned. Stir in turmeric, chili powder, coriander, diced potatoes and salt to taste. Reduce heat, add water, cover and leave on low heat for 15 minutes, stirring occasionally, adding lemon juice during last 5 minutes. Put about 2 tablespoons of the spiced potatoes in the centre of warm dhosai, roll up and serve with a bowl of rasam if desired as a light meal, or as part of an Indian meal.

Spiced Spinach and Lentils

Serves: 4-5

½ cup (4 oz) split red lentils
1½ cups (15 fl oz) cold water
1 bunch spinach, about 500 g (1 lb)
2 tablespoons ghee or oil
1 clove garlic, finely chopped
1 small onion, finely chopped
½ teaspoon ground cummin
½ teaspoon ground coriander
¼ teaspoon chili powder
½ teaspoon garam masala
salt to taste
1 tablespoon lemon juice

Pick over lentils, wash well and place in a pan with the water. Bring to the boil, cover and cook for 30 minutes until soft. Meanwhile wash spinach well, removing roots and any tough stalks. Chop leaves and tender stalks roughly. In a frying pan heat ghee and add garlic and onion. Fry gently until onion is soft, stir in cummin, coriander and chili powder and fry 2 minutes. Add spinach and fry on medium heat until spinach wilts. Pour frying pan contents into lentils, add garam masala, salt to taste and lemon juice. Stir to blend and cook uncovered until mixture is thick. Take care that it does not scorch. Serve hot or warm as a filling for warm dhosai, or over boiled rice as part of an Indian meal.

Stuffed Green Peppers

Serves: 6
Oven temperature: 180°C (350°F)

1 quantity Chick Pea and Rice Stuffing (page 78)
12 medium-sized sweet green bell peppers
boiling, salted water
Tomato Sauce:
1 medium-sized onion, grated
1 clove garlic, crushed
2 tablespoons oil
1 cup (8 fl oz) tomato purée
½ cup (4 fl oz) water
½ teaspoon sugar
salt
freshly ground black pepper
2 tablespoons finely chopped parsley

Make chick pea and rice stuffing according to directions in recipe for Cabbage Rolls with Chick Peas and Rice.

Cut tops from peppers and remove seeds and white membrane. Trim tops and reserve. Wash peppers well and par-boil in boiling water for 5 minutes. Remove peppers and invert to drain. Stand upright in an oiled oven dish and fill loosely with prepared stuffing. Replace tops of peppers.

In a small pan cook onion and garlic in oil for 5 minutes, stir in remaining sauce ingredients and bring to the boil. Pour over peppers in dish. Cover dish with lid or foil and cook in a moderate oven for 45 minutes, remove cover and cook for further 15 minutes, basting peppers if necessary. Serve hot with crusty bread and a side salad.

Mexican Lentils

Serves: 6

2 cups (1 lb) split red lentils
5 cups (2½ cups imperial pints) water
125 g (4 oz) bacon bones or smoked ham hock, cracked
1 large carrot, diced
2 tablespoons lard or oil
1 large onion, chopped
2 cloves garlic, crushed
250 g (8 oz) ripe tomatoes, peeled and chopped
salt
freshly ground black pepper
sour cream for serving

Pick over lentils and wash well. Place in a heavy pan with the water and rinsed bacon bones or hock. Bring to the boil, skimming when necessary. When well-skimmed, add carrots, cover and simmer for 1 hour until lentils are very soft and liquid is reduced. Remove bones or hock and discard. In a frying pan heat lard and add onion. Fry gently until soft, add garlic and cook a few seconds, then add tomatoes. Cook until bubbling and add to lentils with salt and pepper to taste. Leave to cook gently, uncovered, until lentils are thick. Take care that pan contents do not scorch. Serve in deep plates with sour cream served separately to be added to individual taste.

Cabbage Rolls

Serves: 6

Chick Pea and Rice Stuffing:
1½ cups chopped spring onions (scallions)
¼ cup (2 fl oz) olive oil
1 cup (8 oz) long grain rice
1 cup cooked chick peas, drained
½ cup finely chopped parsley
1 cup chopped, peeled tomatoes
½ teaspoon ground allspice
salt
freshly ground black pepper
To finish:
24 cabbage leaves
water
3 cloves garlic
1 teaspoon salt
1 teaspoon dried mint
¼ cup (2 fl oz) lemon juice
½ cup (4 fl oz) olive oil

Gently fry spring onion in ¼ cup olive oil for 2-3 minutes. Turn into a bowl and add remaining stuffing ingredients, adding salt and pepper to taste. Remove leaves from cabbage carefully so as not to tear them, counting larger leaves as 2. Par-boil cabbage leaves in boiling water until limp enough to handle, cooking leaves in 2 or 3 lots. Drain in a colander. Cut out larger part of centre rib in each leaf and cut larger leaves in half down centre. Line the base of a deep pan with ribs and any torn leaves. Place a generous tablespoon of stuffing on base of each leaf, roll up once and tuck in sides to contain filling. Roll to end of leaf.

Repeat with remaining ingredients. Crush garlic with salt and blend in crumbled, crushed mint and lemon juice. Pack rolls flap side down in lined pan, sprinkling some of the garlic-lemon mixture and olive oil between the layers of rolls. Invert a plate on top of the rolls to keep them intact during cooking. Add enough cold water to just cover rolls and put lid on firmly. Bring to the boil on medium heat, reduce to low and simmer gently for 45 minutes. Remove from heat and leave aside for 30 minutes. Serve hot or at room temperature.

Note: Silverbeet (Swiss chard) leaves may be used in place of cabbage. Cut off stems and cut leaves in half if large. Soften by running hot tap water over leaves.

Italian Sausages with Beans

Serves: 6

2 cups (1 lb) cannellini or Great Northern beans
6 cups (3 imperial pints) water
1 bay leaf
1 small onion, quartered
1 small carrot, quartered
salt
500 g (1 lb) fresh Italian sausages
¾ cup (6 fl oz) tomato purée
½ cup (4 fl oz) bean liquid
½ teaspoon sugar
freshly ground black pepper

Wash beans and slow or quick soak according to directions on page 9, using given quantity of water. When plump bring to the boil and add bay leaf, onion and carrot. Cover and boil gently for 1-1½ hours until tender, adding salt to taste after 1 hour.

Prick sausages well and place in a frying pan. Cover with water and bring slowly to the boil. When almost boiling pour off water. Return pan to heat and add oil. Fry sausages gently until browned and cooked through. Remove to a warm platter and keep warm.

Stir tomato purée into fat in pan, cook a little then add the ½ cup bean liquid. Stir in sugar, salt and pepper to taste. Bring to the boil. Drain beans, remove bay leaf, onion and carrot and add beans to tomato sauce. Cover pan and simmer gently for 10 minutes. Place sausages on top of beans, cover and cook for further 5 minutes. Pile beans on platter, put sausages on top and serve with a side salad.

Chick Peas with Spinach

Serves: 6

1½ cups (12 oz) chick peas
5 cups (2½ imperial pints) water
salt
1 large onion, chopped
¼ cup (2 fl oz) olive oil
1 cup (8 fl oz) tomato purée
½ teaspoon sugar
freshly ground black pepper
750 g (1½ lb) spinach

Wash chick peas well and place in a deep pan with the water. Bring to the boil, boil 2 minutes and remove from heat. Cover and leave for 1–2 hours until plump. Return to the boil and boil gently, covered, for 2 hours, adding salt to taste after 1½ hours. Chick peas should be tender after 2 hours.

In a separate pan gently fry onion in oil until transparent. Add tomato purée, sugar and a generous amount of black pepper. Add to the cooked chick peas, cover and leave to simmer while preparing the spinach.

Wash spinach well, removing roots and discoloured leaves. Chop leaves and stems roughly and add to chick peas. Cover and simmer for 20 minutes. Mixture should be moist, not too liquid. If there is too much liquid, remove lid and let mixture boil gently until reduced. Serve as a meal with wholemeal bread, salad and pickles. May be served hot or lukewarm.

Note: Silverbeet (Swiss chard) may be used if spinach is unavailable. Trim off stalks and remove centre rib from leaves. Better stalks may be chopped finely and fried with the onion.

Chick Pea Pilaf

Serves: 6–8

1 cup (8 oz) chick peas
4 cups (2 imperial pints) water
salt
2 cups (1 lb) long grain rice
4 cups (2 imperial pints) chicken stock
3 tablespoons ghee or butter
¼ cup (1 oz) pine nuts (pignolias)
3 small onions
1 teaspoon ground turmeric
2 tablespoons currants

Wash chick peas well, place in a pan and add water. Bring to the boil, boil 2 minutes and remove from heat. Cover and leave aside for 1–2 hours until plump. Return to the boil and simmer, covered, for 1½ hours. Add salt to taste and continue to cook until tender. Drain when cooked.

Meanwhile wash rice in several changes of water until water runs clear. Drain in a sieve, and leave in sieve for at least 30 minutes to dry.

Heat ghee in a deep, heavy pan with well-fitting lid. Add pine nuts and fry, stirring often, until golden brown. Remove to a plate with a draining spoon, leaving ghee in pan. Halve onions lengthwise and slice in semicircles. Add to ghee and fry gently until transparent. Add turmeric, fry for 1 minute, then add rice and stir over medium heat until grains are coated with ghee. Pour in chicken stock and add salt to taste. Bring to the boil quickly, stir well, then reduce heat to low. Put lid on firmly and cook on low heat for 15 minutes.

Scatter currants on top of rice, and top with the drained chick peas. Cover and leave on low heat for further 10 minutes.

Remove lid, put a cloth or white paper towels over rim of pan, replace lid and leave off the heat for 10 minutes. To serve fold currants and chick peas gently through the rice using a fork, and pile on heated dish. Sprinkle pine nuts on top and serve hot with grilled or roast meats or chicken. Also excellent served on its own as a meal, and if served this way pilaf should be accompanied with a bowl of yoghurt at room temperature to be added to individual taste.

Hopping John

Serves: 6

A favourite from the Deep South of North America, where Hopping John eaten on New Year's Day is an assurance of luck for the coming year.

2 cups (1 lb) black-eyed beans
8 cups (4 imperial pints) water
1 tablespoon bacon fat
1 medium-sized onion, chopped
125 g (4 oz) bacon or salt pork in one piece
1 bay leaf
freshly ground black pepper
pinch cayenne pepper
boiling water
1 tablespoon chopped parsley

Wash beans well, put in a pan with water and bring to the boil. Boil 2 minutes, cover and remove from heat. Leave 1 hour until plump. Return to the boil and simmer, covered, for 5 minutes.

Heat bacon fat in a frying pan and add onion. Fry gently until transparent and add to beans with rinsed bacon or salt pork, bay leaf, pepper and cayenne. Cover and cook for 1 hour or until meat is tender and beans almost cooked. Remove meat to a dish, cover and keep warm. Remove bay leaf and discard.

Add rice to beans with 1½ cups boiling water, stir well and return to the boil. Stir again, cover and cook on low heat until rice is tender. Add more boiling water if necessary and stir occasionally during cooking. Drain beans and rice in a colander and turn onto a deep platter. Slice bacon or salt pork and arrange on top of beans and rice. Sprinkle with chopped parsley and serve.

Note: Cooked bacon or salt pork slices may be fried in a greased pan until lightly browned before arranging on bean mixture.

Indian Lentil Cakes

Serves: 6

1½ cups (12 oz) split red lentils or yellow split peas
3 cups (1½ imperial pints) water
1 green chili
1 tablespoon ghee or butter
1 large onion, finely chopped
2 cloves garlic, crushed
1 teaspoon ground turmeric
1 cup finely chopped spinach leaves
2 tablespoons chopped coriander or mint leaves
salt to taste
1 egg, beaten
wholemeal flour or breadcrumbs, optional
To finish:
flour for coating
1 egg, beaten
2 tablespoons milk
dried breadcrumbs
oil or ghee for shallow frying

Pick over lentils or split peas and wash well. Place in a heavy pan with the water and bring to the boil. Skim well, cover and boil gently for 45 minutes. Do not stir while boiling. When soft stir lentils to a purée. If purée holds its shape when stirred, it is thick enough, otherwise cook uncovered, stirring occasionally, until it thickens sufficiently. Turn into a bowl. Seed chili and chop finely.

In a frying pan heat ghee and add onion. Cook on medium heat until transparent, add chili, garlic and turmeric and cook 2 minutes. Stir in spinach and cook until moisture evaporates. Turn frying pan contents into lentil purée, add coriander or mint and salt to taste. Leave until cool.

Blend beaten egg into cooled lentil mixture and chill until firm enough to handle – about 1 hour. If still too soft, blend in 2 to 3 tablespoons wholemeal flour or dried breadcrumbs.

Shape generous tablespoons of mixture into thick patties. Coat with flour, then egg beaten with milk, and finally breadcrumbs. Shallow fry in hot oil or ghee for about 3 minutes each side until golden brown. Drain on paper towels and serve hot with vegetable accompaniment or salad.

Chili Bean Crêpes

Serves: 6

Oven temperature: 180°C (350°F)

These crêpes are filled with refried beans. Either make them following the recipe on page 34, or use a 440g (1 lb) can of refried beans for convenience.

Crêpes:
1 cup (4 oz) plain (all-purpose) flour
pinch salt
1 egg
1 egg yolk
1 tablespoon oil
1¼ cups (½ imperial pint) milk
oil or butter for cooking
Filling:
3 fresh chorizo sausages
2 tablespoons grated sweet green pepper
2 tablespoons chili sauce
½ cup (4 fl oz) tomato purée
salt and pepper
1½ cups Mexican Refried Beans (page 34)
To finish:
1 cup (8 fl oz) sour cream
½ cup (3 oz) grated mild cheddar cheese

Sift flour and salt into a bowl and make a well in the centre. Drop in egg and egg yolk, add oil and half the milk. Stir flour gradually into egg and liquid, and when blended beat until smooth. Gradually beat in remaining milk to give a thin cream consistency. Cover and leave 1 hour. Heat and grease a crêpe pan and pour in enough batter to cover base thinly. Cook until browned on the bottom and top looks dry. Turn and cook further minute. Remove and stack on a plate as crêpes are cooked, and cover with a cloth.

Remove sausage meat from casings and fry meat in a heated pan, stirring to break up lumps. When browned blend in grated pepper, chili sauce, tomato purée and salt and pepper to taste. Simmer 10 minutes.

Spread a heaped tablespoon of refried beans along the centre of each crêpe. Top with same amount of chorizo mixture. Roll up and place in a greased ovenproof dish. Spread cream on top and sprinkle with cheese. Bake in a moderate oven for 15–20 minutes. Serve with a side salad which includes avocado.

Bean and Mushroom Crêpes

Serves: 6

Oven temperature: 180°C (350°F)

1 quantity Crêpes (see above)
2 tablespoons butter
4 spring onions (scallions), chopped
1½ cups (4 oz) sliced mushrooms
1 440g (1 lb) can flageolet or green lima beans
2 tablespoons chopped parsley
salt
freshly ground black pepper
To finish:
½ quantity White Sauce (page 108)
pinch ground nutmeg
2 tablespoons grated Parmesan cheese
paprika

Make and stack crêpes as directed above, cover and keep aside. In a frying pan heat butter and gently fry spring onion for 2 minutes, stir in mushrooms and fry, stirring often, until juices run. Drain beans and add to pan with parsley. Season to taste with salt and pepper. Heat for a few minutes.

Fill crêpes with bean and mushroom mixture, roll up and place in a single layer in a greased ovenproof dish. Make sauce according to directions, stir in nutmeg and pour over crêpes. Sprinkle with cheese and bake in a moderate oven for 15–20 minutes until golden brown. Dust with paprika and serve.

VEGETABLES &SALADS

Though dried bean dishes should be regarded as an important contribution to a meal from a nutritional point of view, some of these recipes are excellent accompaniments. A plump bean salad is perfect for idyllic summer days, and can be a meal in itself. Here you can use canned beans for convenience, so keep a stock on your pantry shelf for those days when you don't want to cook.

Lima Bean Purée

Serves: 6-8
Oven Temperature: 180°C (350°F)

Naturally this dish is from Peru, the home of lima beans. A very simple recipe relying on the pleasant, sweetish flavour and smooth texture of the beans for its appeal.

2 cups (1 lb) large lima beans
6 cups (3 imperial pints) water
salt
2 medium-sized onions, chopped
60 g (2 oz) butter
¼ cup finely chopped parsley
freshly ground black pepper

Wash beans and place in a pan with the water. Bring to the boil, boil 2 minutes and remove from heat. Cover and leave for 2 hours until plump. Return to the boil and cook for 1-1½ hours until tender, adding salt to taste after 1 hour. Drain and purée beans in food processor or vegetable mill, or press through a sieve.

Fry onion gently in butter until transparent. Fold half of the onion into the purée with parsley and pepper to taste. Turn into a buttered casserole dish, swirl with back of a spoon and sprinkle remaining onion on top. Bake in a moderate oven for 20-25 minutes and serve as a vegetable accompaniment.

Vegetables in Chick Pea Flour Batter, page 42.

Tuscan Bean and Tuna Salad

Serves: 6 as a meal, 10-12 as an appetizer

A popular addition to the Florentine antipasto platter, or serve as a light lunch.

2 cups (1 lb) borlotti, saluggia or cannellini beans
6 cups (3 imperial pints) water
salt
1 medium-sized onion
1 x 220 g (7 oz) can tuna (tunny fish) in oil
Italian Dressing:
½ cup (4 fl oz) olive oil
¼ cup lemon juice
1 crushed clove garlic
salt to taste
freshly ground black pepper
2 mashed anchovy fillets, optional

Wash beans well, place in a pan and add water. Bring to the boil, boil 2 minutes and remove from heat. Cover and leave for 1-2 hours until plump. Return to the boil and cook for 1½-3 hours, depending on bean used, until tender but still intact. Add salt to taste towards end of cooking. Drain and cool. Halve onion lengthwise and cut out root. Slice into slender wedges to make gently curved slivers of onion. Mix into beans and pile beans in a bowl.

Drain tuna and gently break fish into neat, longish flakes. Pile in centre of beans. Make dressing by shaking ingredients in a screw top jar, omitting salt if anchovy fillets are used. Pour over beans and tuna, cover and chill for 2 hours. Toss at table.

USING CANNED BEANS: Replace cooked dried beans with 3 300 g (10 oz) or 2 440 g (1 lb) cans borlotti (Roman), cannellini or Great Northern beans.

Bean Sprout-Watercress Salad

Serves: 6

¼ cup (2 fl oz) salad oil
2 tablespoons cider vinegar
1 teaspoon finely chopped fresh ginger
1 clove garlic, finely chopped
2 teaspoons soya sauce
1 teaspoon salt
freshly ground black pepper
large bunch watercress
2 cups (8 oz) bean sprouts
2 tablespoons sesame seeds, toasted

Combine oil in a jar with vinegar, ginger, garlic, salt and pepper. Shake well then leave aside for 2 hours or more. Wash watercress well and break into neat sprigs — about 5-6 cups watercress will be required. Shake dry and wrap loosely in a cloth. Put into a large plastic bag and leave in refrigerator until required. Rinse bean sprouts under cold water, remove loose skins and nip off any browned ends. Drain well, roll in another cloth, place in plastic bag and refrigerate. Toast sesame seeds in a heavy pan over medium heat until golden brown and remove to a dish.

Just before serving shake dressing well and strain into salad bowl. Add watercress and bean sprouts, toss well and sprinkle with toasted sesame seeds.

Three Bean Salad, page 89, Lupini, page 39; and Tuscan Bean and Tuna Salad, above.

Bean and Vegetable Salad

Serves: 6

2 cups (1 lb) large lima, cannellini or Great Northern beans
water
1 cup cooked fresh green peas
1 cup sliced celery
½ cup finely chopped white onion
1 cup chopped green and red sweet pepper
1 cup diced carrot, lightly boiled and still crisp
salt
freshly ground black pepper
2 tablespoons snipped chives
Dressing:
½ cup good mayonnaise
½ cup sour cream
1 tablespoon white vinegar
½ teaspoon prepared English mustard

Wash beans well, cover with 6-7 cups water and soak overnight in a cool place. Drain, add fresh water to cover and bring to the boil. Boil gently, covered, for 1½ hours or until tender but not broken. Drain and combine with remaining vegetables (not chives) and add salt and pepper to taste. Cover and chill thoroughly.

Combine dressing ingredients and mix into salad, turn into a bowl and sprinkle with snipped chives. Chill until required.

STUFFED TOMATOES
Prepare above salad and chill. Wash 12 firm, ripe tomatoes of even size, cut off stem end neatly and scoop our flesh using a potato baller. Set tomatoes upside down on a rack to drain. Sprinkle inside tomatoes with salt and a little sugar and fill with bean salad, piling it high. Put a sprig of watercress or parsley on top of each and arrange on a flat platter. Serve chilled. Remaining salad may be served separately.

USING CANNED BEANS: Replace cooked dried beans with 2 440 g (1 lb) cans three-bean mix.

Chick Pea and Eggplant Stew

Serves: 6

A Middle East favourite, particularly in Lebanon and Syria, and served with flat Arab bread as a main meal. However it may be served as a hot vegetable accompaniment, or cold 'salad'.

1½ cups (12 oz) chick peas
5 cups water
2 medium sized oval eggplants
salt
1 large onion, chopped
1 clove garlic, crushed
⅓ cup (3 fl oz) olive oil
500 g (1 lb) ripe tomatoes, peeled and chopped
salt
freshly ground black pepper
2 tablespoons chopped parsley

Wash chick peas well, place in a deep pan with the water and bring to the boil. Boil 2 minutes, remove from heat, cover and leave aside for 1 hour until plump. Return to the boil, skimming when necessary. Cover and boil gently for 2 hours or until tender. Drain, reserving some of the liquid. Leave chick peas in pan.

Meanwhile wash eggplant and cut into 2 cm (¾ inch) rounds. Quarter each round to give wedges. Skin should be left on. Sprinkle liberally with salt and leave aside for 30 minutes. Rinse and dry with paper towels. In a frying pan heat half the oil, add onion and fry gently until soft, add garlic and cook a few seconds then pour into chick peas. Add remaining oil to pan, add eggplant pieces and fry over high heat, turning eggplant gently with a wooden spoon to brown lightly and evenly without cooking it completely. Add to chick peas with tomatoes, salt and pepper to taste and half the parsley.

If mixture looks too dry add ½ cup reserved liquid from chick peas, cover and simmer gently for 20 minutes until eggplant is cooked but still intact. Serve hot piled in a dish and sprinkle with remaining parsley. Also good served at room temperature or chilled.

Red Kidney Beans Bourguingnon

Serves: 6

2 cups (1lb) red kidney beans
6 cups (3 imperial pints) water
bouquet garni
1 small onion, finely chopped
salt
freshly ground black pepper
125 g (4 oz) fatty bacon
8-12 button onions
1 cup (8 fl oz) dry red wine
1 tablespoon butter
1½ tablespoons plain flour
1 tablespoon finely chopped parsley

Wash beans well, place in a pan with the water and bring to the boil. Boil 2 minutes, remove from heat, cover and leave for 1 hour until plump. Return to the boil, add bouquet garni and chopped onion, cover and boil gently for 1½ hours or until just tender but still intact. Drain, reserving liquid. Remove bouquet garni and add salt and pepper to taste. Remove skin from bacon if present and cut bacon into dice. Place in a heated frying pan and fry until crisp.

Remove bacon with a slotted spoon and add to beans. Peel onions and cut a cross in root end to prevent centres popping out. Add to fat in pan and cook until lightly browned. Add wine, stir to lift browned sediment, then add to beans. Mix gently to combine and add about ½ cup reserved bean liquid. Cover and simmer gently for 30 minutes, adding a little more liquid if necessary. After cooking there should be about 1 cup liquid left. Blend butter with flour and stir bit by bit into beans until sauce thickens. Boil gently for 2 minutes and serve piled in a dish and sprinkled with chopped parsley.

Indonesian Salad with Peanut Sauce

Serves: 6

2 small potatoes
1 medium-sized carrot
¼ small cauliflower broken into florets
125 g (4 oz) green beans, sliced diagonally
1 cup (4 oz) bean sprouts
1 small sweet green pepper
1 small sweet red pepper
2 stalks celery
1 cucumber
1 quantity Peanut Sauce (page 103)

Scrub potatoes and boil in their skins; peel, dice and cool. Scrape carrot and cut in matchstick sized pieces. Par-boil carrot sticks, cauliflower and beans in salted water, cooking each lot separately. Cook until just tender – they should still be crisp. As each vegetable is cooked, strain in a colander and run cold water over it. Drain and cool thoroughly. Chill the cooked vegetables. Wash bean sprouts, nip off any browned tips and remove any skins. Drain well. Wash peppers, celery and cucumbers well. Clean peppers and cut into strips; slice celery or cut into short lengths; score skin on cucumber with a fork and slice thinly.

Arrange prepared vegetables on a platter in groups, and serve with peanut sauce in a separate bowl. A good accompaniment to pork and beef satays.

Note: Any combination of vegetables may be used. Watercress sprigs, shredded, blanched cabbage or radishes are other suitable ingredients, and for a complete salad meal add quartered hard-boiled eggs.

Hot Bean Salad

Serves: 6

1½ cups (12 oz) Great Northern or cannellini beans
5 cups (2½ imperial pints) water
salt
175 g (6 oz) streaky bacon
1 onion, finely chopped
4 spring onions (scallions), chopped
2 tablespoons chopped parsley
1 tablespoon oil
3 tablespoons wine vinegar
freshly ground black pepper

Wash beans, place in a pan with the water and bring to the boil. Boil 2 minutes, remove from heat, cover and leave for 1 hour until plump. Alternatively beans may be slow-soaked for several hours – a better method for salad beans as the skins are less likely to come off during cooking. If slow soaked, drain off water and add fresh water to cover. Bring plumped beans to the boil and boil gently for 1½ hours or until tender, adding salt to taste after 1 hour.

Remove skin from bacon if present and dice bacon. Put into a heated frying pan and fry until fat is rendered and bacon is browned and crisp. Add onion and cook on low heat until soft. Drain beans and place in a bowl. Add frying pan contents, including the bacon fat, spring onion, parsley, oil, vinegar and pepper to taste. Toss well and serve hot as a vegetable accompaniment.

USING CANNED BEANS: Replace cooked dried beans with 2 440 g (1 lb) cans soya or other white beans. Heat thoroughly, drain and finish as above.

Three Bean Salad

Serves: 6-8

A popular Italian bean salad, so popular that canners prepare it as part of their canned bean range. A dried three-bean mix is also widely available and usually comprises of baby green lima, cannellini or Great Northern, and red kidney beans. These three beans usually cook in the same time; if another selection is required, it might be necessary to cook each type separately. Of course three varieties of canned beans may be used for convenience.

2 cups (1 lb) three-bean mix or your own selection of beans
6 cups (3 imperial pints) water
salt
4 spring onions (scallions)
1 sweet green pepper, diced
1 sweet red pepper, diced
1 quantity Italian Dressing (page 85)

Wash beans well and place in a pan with the water. Bring to the boil, boil 2 minutes and remove from heat. Cover and leave for 1 hour until plump. Return to the boil and cook for 1-1½ hours until tender, adding salt to taste after 1 hour. When cooked drain in colander and turn into a bowl.

Clean spring onions, retaining some of the green tops. Chop onions and tops and add to warm beans with diced peppers. Make dressing according to directions, omitting anchovies. Cider or wine vinegar may replace the lemon juice if desired. Pour over salad, toss lightly, cover and chill for at least 4 hours so that beans absorb the dressing. Turn into a clean salad bowl and serve.

USING CANNED BEANS: Replace cooked dried beans with 2 440 g (1 lb) cans three-bean mix.

Lentil Salad

Serves: 6

1½ cups (12 oz) brown (continental) lentils
4 cups (2 imperial pints) water
1 bay leaf
1 small onion, chopped
1 teaspoon salt
3 spring onions (scallions)
1 dill pickled cucumber, diced
2 tablespoons chopped parsley
½ quantity French Dressing (page 92)

Pick over lentils, wash well and place in a pan with the water. Bring to the boil and skim well. Add bay leaf and chopped onion and reduce heat. Cover pan and boil gently for 30–45 minutes until lentils are tender but intact. Remove bay leaf, drain lentils in a colander and turn into a bowl. Cover and chill.

Slice spring onions, including some green tops, and mix into lentils with diced cucumber and half the parsley. Make dressing according to directions (or use about ⅓ cup bottled dressing), pour over salad, toss well and sprinkle remaining parsley on top.

Lentil and Rice Pilaf

Serves: 6

A popular pilaf from the Middle East. Traditionally the brown or green lentils are soaked and the husks removed by rubbing handfuls of lentils together. The husks are floated off with water and the process repeated until all are cleaned. Rather a time consuming process and not really necessary as the husks contribute valuable fibre to the diet. While the ratio of water to rice and lentils is much less than normally used, the pilaf is steamed slowly rather than boiled.

½ cup brown or green lentils
2 cups (1 lb) long grain rice, preferably basmati rice
2 medium-sized onions
¼ cup (2 oz) ghee (clarified butter)
4 cups (2 imperial pints) water
salt

Pick over lentils and place in a bowl. Cover with water and remove any that float. Wash lentils well, add 2 cups water and leave to soak for 1–2 hours. Drain well.

If using basmati rice, pick over to remove any small stones. Wash rice in several changes of water to remove starch and drain well.

In a deep pan heat half the ghee and add 1 sliced onion. Fry until golden brown and remove to a plate with a slotted spoon. Keep aside.

Add remaining ghee to pan with second onion, finely chopped. Fry on medium heat until transparent and lightly flecked with brown. Add rice and lentils and stir over heat for 3 minutes. Add boiling water and about 2 teaspoons salt. Return to the boil, stirring occasionally. Reduce heat to low, cover pan and simmer gently for 45 minutes. Do not stir during this time.

When lentils and rice are tender, remove lid and place 2 paper towels or a cloth over rim of pan. Replace lid firmly and leave pilaf off the heat for 10–15 minutes. Pile pilaf in a dish with the browned onion rings strewn on top. Serve as an accompaniment to grilled or baked meat, fish or chicken.

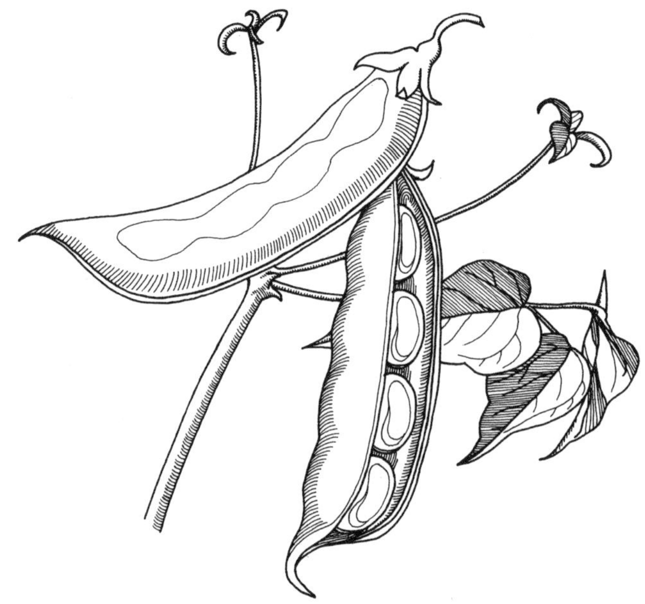

Creamed Butter Beans

Serves: 6-8
Oven Temperature: 180°C (350°F)

2 cups (1 lb) butter beans
6 cups water
2 cups (1 imperial pint) milk
1 bay leaf
blade of mace
1 onion studded with 2 cloves
1 carrot, quartered
½ cup (4 fl oz) cream
salt
freshly ground white pepper
2 tablespoons butter
1 tablespoon grated Parmesan cheese

Wash beans well, place in a pan and add water. Bring to the boil and boil for 2 minutes. Remove from heat, cover and leave aside for 2 hours until plump. Drain off 2 cups liquid and add the milk, bay leaf, mace, clove-studded onion and carrot. Return to the boil, cover and cook on low heat for 1½ hours until beans are very soft and most of liquid is absorbed. Remove carrot, onion, bay leaf and mace. Mash beans with potato masher or purée in food processor in 2 batches. Blend in cream and salt and pepper to taste.

Grease an oven dish with a little of the butter and spread purée in dish. Dot top with butter and sprinkle with cheese. Bake in a moderate oven for 30 minutes or until top is lightly browned. Serve hot as a vegetable accompaniment to roast pork, grilled pork chops or other roast or grilled meats.

Stir-Fried Bean Sprouts

Serves: 4

2 cups (8 oz) bean sprouts
3 spring onions (scallions)
2 tablespoons peanut oil
1 clove garlic, crushed
1 tablespoon finely shredded fresh ginger
1 teaspoon soya sauce
salt to taste

Rinse bean sprouts under cold water, remove any loose skins and nip off any browned tails. Drain well. Cut spring onions in 3 cm (1¼ inch) lengths, including better green tops.

Heat oil in a wok and add garlic and ginger. Stir-fry for 30 seconds then add bean sprouts. Stir-fry for 1 minute, add spring onion and fry for further minute. Add soya sauce and salt to taste, toss well and serve immediately.

Spinach and Lima Bean Salad

Serves: 6

Try to use spinach if available, otherwise choose tender young silverbeet (Swiss chard) leaves. I prefer the baby green limas for this salad. If you cannot obtain them in dried form, used canned lima beans.

2½-3 cups cooked green lima beans (see page 16) or 3 300 g (10 oz) cans lima beans
1 bunch spinach or tender silverbeet (Swiss chard)
125 g (4 oz) bacon slices
4 spring onions, chopped
French Dressing
½ teaspoon dry mustard
¼ teaspoon salt
½ cup (4 fl oz) olive oil
2 tablespoons wine or cider vinegar
1 clove garlic
freshly ground pepper to taste

Cook the lima beans, adding salt to taste after 1 hour's boiling. Drain and cool. Wash spinach or silverbeet well. Remove stalks from leaves; if using silverbeet cut out white centre ribs. Drain leaves, wrap in a tea towel and place in refrigerator for 2 hours to crisp them. If not to be used immediately, place wrapped leaves in a plastic bag.

Remove skin from bacon if present. Chop bacon into small squares and place in a heated frying pan. Stir occasionally over medium heat until crisp. Drain off fat and remove bacon to paper towels to drain completely.

Tear spinach or silverbeet into bite-sized pieces and place in salad bowl. Add beans and spring onions. Sprinkle bacon on top and pour about ¼ cup French dressing over salad just before serving. Toss at the table.

To make French Dressing: Blend mustard powder with salt to break up lumps. Put into a screw top jar with oil, vinegar, bruised or crushed garlic and pepper to taste. Shake well. If bruised garlic is used, let dressing stand for 1 hour, remove garlic and shake again just before using. Store remaining dressing in jar at room temperature.

Bean Curd and Sprout Salad

Serves: 6

6 pieces compressed bean curd (page 19)
oil for deep frying
1½ cups (6 oz) bean sprouts
2 small cucumbers
4–6 radishes
½ quantity Peanut Sauce (page 103)
1 tablespoon lemon juice
water

If you cannot buy compressed bean curd, then take 6 pieces fresh bean curd, each about 5 cm (2 inches) square and place on a cloth-lined flat dish, spacing pieces apart. Top with another cloth and put a board on top of the bean curd. Weigh down evenly with a heavy object and leave for 1-2 hours until half original thickness. Wipe dry when compressed.

Heat oil and deep fry compressed bean curd until golden. This takes about 4-5 minutes, frying 3 pieces at a time. Drain on paper towels, cut into 1 cm (½ inch) slices and leave until cool.

Rinse bean sprouts under cold water, nip off any browned ends and remove any husks. Drain well. Choose young, firm cucumbers, wash, dry and score skin with a fork. Slice thinly. Wash radishes and slice thinly.

Make Peanut Sauce as directed, cool thoroughly then thin down with lemon juice and enough water to give a thick cream consistency.

Arrange cucumber and radish slices on individual salad plates and put bean curd slices on top. Scatter bean sprouts over the bean curd and pour some of the sauce over the top, serving remainder separately.

Mixed Bean Salad

Serves: 6-8

Use freshly cooked beans for economy or canned beans for convenience. While I have specified certain beans here, the combination may be changed according to ingredients on hand with an eye to colour and shape variation. Refer to bean types in front of book for cooking times.

1½ cups cooked red kidney beans
1½ cups cooked baby green or white lima beans
1½ cups cooked cannellini or Great Northern beans
1½ cups cooked chick peas
250 g (8 oz) fresh green beans
1 cup chopped spring onions (scallions)
1 inner celery stalk, sliced
1 clove garlic, crushed
1 teaspoon chopped fresh dill
2 tablespoons chopped parsley
salt
freshly ground black pepper
½ cup (4 fl oz) French dressing (page 92)

Drain cooked beans well and combine in a bowl. Top and tail fresh beans, cut into 2 cm (¾ inch) lengths and cook in boiling, salted water for 5 minutes, drain and run cold water through them. Add to cooked beans with remaining ingredients. Toss well, cover and chill for at least 2 hours. Toss again and pile into a bowl lined with crisp lettuce leaves.

Succotash

Serves: 6
Oven temperature: 180°C (350°F)

1 cup (8 oz) baby green lima beans
3 cups (1½ imperial pints) water
salt
2 cups (12 oz) canned or frozen corn kernels
freshly ground white pepper
¼ cup (2 fl oz) cream
¼ cup (2 fl oz) milk
¼ cup (2 oz) butter

Wash beans well, add water and bring to the boil. Boil 2 minutes, remove from heat, cover and leave for 1 hour. Return to the boil and cook, covered, for 1-1½ hours until tender, adding salt to taste towards end of cooking.

Drain canned corn; if using frozen corn, boil in salted water until tender, then drain.

When beans are cooked, drain and add corn to beans. Turn into a casserole dish and stir in cream and milk. Dot top with butter and reheat in a moderate oven for 20 minutes. Stir towards end of cooking. Serve as a vegetable accompaniment.

USING CANNED BEANS: Replace cooked dried beans with 2 300 g (10 oz) cans lima beans. Heat thoroughly, drain and proceed with recipe.

Turkish White Bean Salad

PIYAZ

Serves: 6-8

2 cups (1 lb) dried haricot (navy) or other white beans
6 cups (3 imperial pints) cold water
salt
1 clove garlic
2 small onions
¼ cup chopped parsley
1 teaspoon chopped fresh mint
2 teaspoons chopped dill
¼ cup (2 fl oz) lemon juice
1 tablespoon white vinegar
¼ cup (2 fl oz) olive oil
¼ cup (2 fl oz) good salad oil
To finish:
1 sweet green pepper
3 hard-boiled eggs

Wash beans well, place in a pan with the water and bring to the boil. Boil 2 minutes, remove from heat, cover and leave aside until plump. Return beans to the boil, cover and simmer gently until tender but still intact. Cooking time will vary according to type of bean used. Add salt to taste after 1½ hours cooking. When tender drain well and turn into a bowl.

Crush garlic with a little salt. Halve onions lengthwise then slice thinly into semicircles. Add to hot beans with lemon juice, vinegar and combined oils. Leave until cool. Gently mix in chopped herbs and chill salad for 1-2 hours. Serve in a deep bowl garnished with sliced green pepper and sliced or quartered hard-boiled eggs.

Sprout and Peanut Salad

Serves: 6

4 cups (1 lb) bean sprouts
4 spring onions (scallions)
2 tablespoons chopped coriander leaves
Peanut Dressing:
¼ cup crunchy peanut butter
¼ cup soya sauce
2 teaspoons cider vinegar
1 teaspoon brown sugar
1 clove garlic, crushed
¼ teaspoon ground turmeric
⅛–¼ teaspoon chili powder
2–3 tablespoons water
2 tablespoons peanut oil

Nip off any browned ends from sprouts. Rinse well in cold water and remove any bean husks present. Drain well in a colander, wrap in a tea towel and place in a plastic bag. Chill until required.

Clean spring onions, retaining better green tops. Slice onions and tops diagonally, keeping slices as thin as possible. Place in a bowl with the bean sprouts and toss lightly. Prepare dressing, pour over salad, toss lightly and chill until required for serving. Sprinkle coriander over salad and serve.

To make Peanut Dressing: Blend dressing ingredients in a bowl, adding chili powder to taste and enough water to thin down to a pouring consistency. Leave at room temperature until required.

Yam and Peanut Croquettes

Makes about 24

2 cups mashed yam or sweet potato
2 cups (8 oz) finely ground roasted peanuts
grated rind of 1 orange
salt to taste
pinch cayenne pepper
dried breadcrumbs
1 egg
2 tablespoons milk
oil for deep-frying

For 2 cups mashed yam or sweet potato you will require whole yams or sweet potatoes weighing about 600 g (1¼ lb). Scrub and boil in their skins in salted water to cover, cooking for 25–30 minutes until tender. Drain, cool and peel off skin. Mash with a fork.

Put mashed yam into a mixing bowl with ground peanuts, orange rind, salt to taste and the cayenne. Blend thoroughly, and if too soft to handle, blend in 2 tablespoons flour. Shape generous tablespoons of mixture into croquettes. Roll in breadcrumbs, coat with egg beaten with milk, and roll again in breadcrumbs. Deep-fry in hot oil, cooking 5–6 at a time. Drain on paper towels. Serve hot as a vegetable accompaniment to roast or grilled pork or chicken. Very good as a side dish for roast turkey.

Asparagus Bean Casserole

Serves: 6

1 cup (8 oz) lima or butter beans
3 cups (1½ imperial pints) water
1 carrot, quartered
1 small onion
1 bay leaf
salt
1 425 g can green asparagus cuts
freshly ground black pepper
½ quantity White Sauce (page 108)
½ cup (2 oz) soft breadcrumbs
1 tablespoon grated Parmesan cheese

Wash beans and quick soak as directed on page 9 . When plump add carrot, onion and bay leaf and bring to the boil. Boil, covered, for 1–1½ hours until tender, adding salt to taste after 1 hour. Drain and remove carrot, onion and bay leaf.

Drain asparagus and add to beans with pepper to taste. Make white sauce according to directions and fold ½ cup sauce into beans and asparagus. Turn into a greased casserole dish and spread remaining sauce on top. Toss breadcrumbs in melted butter, mix in cheese and sprinkle on top of casserole. Bake in a moderate oven for 25–30 minutes until golden brown. Serve as an accompaniment to meat or chicken. For a light meal add 4 quartered hard-boiled eggs to beans and asparagus and serve with a side salad.

USING CANNED BEANS: Replace cooked dried beans with 2 300 g (10 oz) cans lima or butter beans. Omit carrot, onion and bay leaf. Heat beans, drain and proceed with recipe.

Lima Bean and Fennel Salad

Serves: 6

1½ cups (12 oz) small white or green lima beans
4 cups (2 imperial pints) water
salt
2 fennel bulbs
3 spring onions (scallions), chopped
1 tablespoon chopped fennel leaves
fennel sprigs

Dressing:
1 clove garlic
½ teaspoon salt
¼ cup (2 fl oz) olive oil
1 tablespoon white vinegar
1 tablespoon lemon juice
freshly ground black pepper

Wash beans and slow soak for several hours as directed on page 9 . Drain and add given quantity of water. Bring to the boil and boil gently for 1 hour until tender, adding salt to taste after 45 minutes. Drain, turn into a bowl, cover and chill.

Wash fennel bulbs, trim and cut into thin strips a little thicker than a matchstick. Add to chilled beans with finely chopped spring onion and pour on prepared dressing. Toss lightly and sprinkle chopped fennel leaves on top. Garnish with sprigs of fennel.

To make dressing: Crush garlic to a paste with salt. Put into a screw top jar, add oil, vinegar, lemon juice and a generous amount of pepper. Seal and shake well. Pour over salad just before serving.

Bean and Apple Salad

Serves: 4–6

1 cup (8 oz) Great Northern or white lima beans
3 cups (1½ imperial pints) water
salt
3 crisp red apples
lemon juice
1 cup sliced celery
½ cup (4 fl oz) bottled mayonnaise
¼ cup (2 fl oz) sour cream
½ cup (3 oz) shelled roasted peanuts

Wash and slow soak beans according to directions on page 9 . Drain, add given quantity of water and bring to the boil. Boil gently, covered, for 1–1½ hours or until tender, adding salt to taste after 45 minutes. Drain and chill.

Halve and core apples. Do not peel. Cut one half into slender wedges, dice the remainder, keeping sliced and diced apples separately. Sprinkle lemon juice over apples, toss to coat and add diced apples to beans. Add celery, toss lightly and turn into a salad bowl.

Blend mayonnaise and sour cream and pour over salad. Arrange sliced apple around edge of salad and sprinkle husked peanuts on top. Toss at the table and serve on its own as a separate salad course, or as a meal with cold ham or chicken.

USING CANNED BEANS: Replace cooked dried beans with 2 300 g (10 oz) cans soya, lima or other white beans. Soya beans will require heating before draining is possible.

Roman Bean and Ham Salad

Serves: 4–6

1½ cups (12 oz) borlotti (Roman) beans
4 cups (2 imperial pints) water
salt
½ sweet red pepper
½ sweet green pepper
1 medium-sized onion
175 g (6 oz) thickly sliced ham
1 quantity Italian Dressing (page 85)
3 medium-sized tomatoes, peeled
2 teaspoons chopped fresh basil

Wash and slow soak beans according to directions on page 9 . Drain, add given quantity of fresh water and bring to the boil. Cover and boil gently for 1½–2 hours until tender, adding salt after 1 hour. Drain and chill.

Seed peppers and dice. Halve onion lengthwise and slice into slender wedges. Dice ham. Add peppers, onion and ham to beans and toss lightly.

Make Italian dressing as directed in recipe for Tuscan Bean and Tuna Salad, replacing lemon juice with vinegar and omitting anchovies. Pour all but 2 tablespoons of the dressing over salad and toss lightly. Chill until required.

Turn salad into a deep platter piling it in the centre. Cut tomatoes in wedges and arrange around edge of salad. Trickle remaining dressing over tomatoes and sprinkle tomatoes with basil. If fresh basil is not available, soak 1 teaspoon dried basil leaves in the reserved dressing for 10 minutes, then pour onto tomatoes.

USING CANNED BEANS: Replace cooked dried beans with 2 300 g (10 oz) cans borlotti (Roman) beans. This quantity serves 4.

Red Bean and Chicken Salad

Serves: 6

3 cups diced cooked chicken
1 345 g (11 oz) can mandarin orange sections
1 440 g (1 lb) can red kidney beans
1 cup sliced celery
2 medium-sized onions, sliced
crisp lettuce leaves
salt to taste
Honey Dressing:
3 tablespoons oil
1 tablespoon fresh orange juice
1 tablespoon fresh lemon juice
1 tablespoon honey
½ teaspoon ground ginger
¼ teaspoon salt
freshly ground black pepper

Remove skin and bones from chicken before dicing and measuring. Drain mandarin orange sections and beans and place in a bowl with chicken. Add celery and 1 sliced onion separated into rings. Add salt to taste and toss lightly. Make dressing and pour over salad. Toss again and chill thoroughly.

When ready to serve line a salad bowl or individual salad plates with crisp lettuce leaves. Pile salad on top. Separate remaining onion slices into rings and arrange over salad.

To make Honey Dressing: Put all ingredients in a bowl and beat with a fork until combined. Beat again before pouring onto salad.

SOMETHING EXTRA . . .

When looking at the bean cooking of different countries there is always something extra which must be served with or included in the dish for authenticity. An Indian meal without chapatis, Mexican beans without tortillas, Minestrone Genoese without Pesto Sauce – never! You will also discover the delights of being able to prepare your own peanut butter, bean curd and bean sprouts. Very satisfying!

Chapatis

Makes: 10-12

1½ cups (6 oz) wholemeal flour
1 teaspoon salt
3 teaspoons oil
½ cup (4 fl oz) tepid water
oil or ghee for cooking

Combine flour and salt in a bowl, make a well and add oil and most of water into centre of flour. Gradually stir flour into liquid until combined, then knead by hand, adding more water if dough is too dry. Knead vigorously for 10 minutes. If dough is very soft, the kneading will develop the gluten, thus absorbing more moisture. Divide into even sized portions, rolling each into smooth balls. Roll out on a lightly floured board until very thin, about 15 cm (6 inches) in diameter. Place chapatis on a cloth and cover with another cloth until all are rolled.

Heat a flat griddle or heavy frying pan on medium heat and grease with a wad of paper towel dipped in ghee or oil. Starting with the first chapati rolled out, place in pan and cook until golden brown on base, pressing edges gently with a folded cloth. Turn and cook other side, again pressing if necessary. When cooked wrap in a cloth to keep warm while remainder are cooked. Stack the cooked chapatis in the cloth. Serve warm with Indian meals.

Pesto Sauce

Though traditionally made in a mortar, with ingredients painstakingly pounded with a pestle, the food processor makes short work of this classic sauce from Genoa. It is a pasta sauce, but does wonders for Minestrone, or simply tossed through hot boiled white beans.

1 cup (2 oz) coarsely chopped fresh basil leaves
3-4 cloves garlic, chopped
⅓ cup (2 oz) pine nuts (pignolias)
½ cup (2 oz) grated Parmesan cheese
60 g (2 oz) young Pecorino Romano cheese or packaged cream cheese at room temperature
½ cup olive oil

Put all ingredients except oil in food processor bowl with steel blade fitted. Process until well combined, scraping down sides of bowl when necessary. When thick, with basil well blended into ingredients, pour oil in a thin stream through feeder tube while processor is in action. Stop action as soon as last of oil is added. Pile into a bowl and serve as directed in recipes.

Corn Bread

Oven Temperature: 200°C (400°F)

1½ cups (6 oz) plain (all purpose) flour
4 teaspoons baking powder
3 teaspoons caster (fine) sugar
½ teaspoon salt
1½ cups (9 oz) yellow cornmeal (polenta)
2 eggs
1¼ cups (10 fl oz) milk
⅓ cup (3 oz) melted, cooled butter

Sift flour with baking powder into a bowl and stir in sugar, salt and cornmeal. Beat eggs and add to dry ingredients with milk. Stir until combined and beat in melted butter. Pour into a greased slab cake pan, 18 x 28cm (7 x 11 inches). Spread out evenly and bake in a hot oven for 30 minutes. Cut into squares and serve warm with Chili Con Carne or other bean meals.

Vegetable Stock

(VEGETARIAN COOKING)

Keeping liquid from boiled vegetables is a common culinary practice as it adds flavour and nutritional value to soups, stews and sauces. However in the vegetarian cooking of beans where vegetable stock is substituted for meat flavours, such liquid is unsuitable because of the salt content (unless it is added after the beans have cooked for some time). This vegetable stock should prove useful for those who practice vegetarianism.

500 g (1 lb) carrots
1 outer celery stalk, with leaves
1 large onion, chopped
1 sweet green pepper, cleaned and chopped
4 sprigs parsley
1 bay leaf
Additional vegetables: **(some of the following)**
outer leaves of cabbage, cauliflower leaves, green tops of leeks and spring onions (scallions), zucchini and marrow trimmings, green bean trimmings, green pea shells, broccoli leaves, spinach stems and roots, silverbeet (Swiss chard) stems
water to cover

Wash and chop vegetables. Only remove skins where necessary. Remove stem, seeds and white membrane from pepper. With trimmings from such vegetables as beans, zucchini and marrow, be sure to wash vegetables well before initial preparation, not afterwards. Outer leaves of cabbage, cauliflower and broccoli leaves must be well washed in several changes of water to remove any pesticide residue. Put vegetables and herbs in a large pan and cover well with water. Bring to the boil and boil gently, covered, for 1 hour. Strain into suitable containers and cool. Seal and store in coldest part of refrigerator for up to 3 days; in freezer for long term storage. Use as a basis for bean soups, stews and for sauces.

Onion Sambal

2 medium-sized brown onions
salt
2 teaspoons dark brown sugar
2 tablespoons lemon juice
1 teaspoon finely chopped fresh ginger
1–2 fresh red chilis
2 tablespoons chopped coriander leaves

Slice onions thinly, place in a bowl and sprinkle generously with salt. Cover and leave 1 hour. Press down on onion with fist to release moisture, then drain off liquid. Rinse quickly with cold water and drain well. Put into a bowl and add sugar, lemon juice, ginger, seeded and thinly sliced chili and coriander leaves. Toss well, cover and chill until required. Serve as directed in recipes, and as a side dish to Indian pulse dishes such as Dhal, Spiced Black Gram Purée and Dhal with Cabbage.

Indonesian Salad with Peanut Sauce, page 88.

Peanut Butter

Makes: about 2 cups

500 g (1 lb) shelled, unsalted, roasted peanuts
⅓ cup (3 fl oz) peanut or polyunsaturated oil
½ teaspoon salt or to taste

Rub skins off peanuts if present. Put nuts into food processor fitted with steel blade and process until ground. Gradually add oil and process until oil is absorbed and a paste is formed. Add salt to taste and store in a sealed jar.

Note: The food processor gives a crunchy textured peanut butter. For a smooth texture, put half the peanuts and all of the oil in a blender jar and blend until smooth. Gradually add remaining peanuts until a smooth paste is formed. Of course you can stop blending before this stage for crunchy peanut butter if you have no food processor.

Peanut Sauce

Makes: about 1½ cups

1 cup (6 oz) roasted peanuts
1-2 fresh red chilis
1 teaspoon dried shrimp paste or anchovy sauce, optional
2 tablespoons peanut oil
1 medium-sized onion, finely chopped
1 clove garlic, crushed
1 cup (8 fl oz) thick coconut milk (page 105)
4 teaspoons dark soya sauce
2 teaspoons brown sugar
2-3 teaspoons lemon juice
salt to taste

Remove skins from peanuts by rubbing in a cloth. Coarsely grind peanuts in nut grinder or food processor. Halve chilis lengthwise and remove seeds and white membrane. Chop very finely or pound to a paste using pestle and mortar. Heat oil in pan and fry onion gently for 5 minutes until soft, add chili and garlic and fry for further 3 minutes. Add coconut milk and bring to the boil. Stir in prepared peanuts and cook for further 3 minutes until sauce thickens. Cool and serve as directed in recipes. Serve hot as a sauce for beef and pork satays.
Note: If sauce is too thick when cooled, blend in thin coconut milk or water until sauce drops off the end of a spoon. To prepare this sauce more quickly, 1 cup crunchy peanut butter may be used instead of the roasted peanuts.

Stir-Fried Pork and Bean Sprouts, page 54, with popular Asian 'offshoots' – salted black beans, Bean Sprouts, page 109, soya sauce and Bean Curd, page 107.

Aioli

Makes: about 2 cups

6 cloves garlic
salt
3 teaspoons lemon juice
3 egg yolks
1½ cups (12 fl oz) olive oil
cold water, optional
white pepper to taste

Pound garlic and about ½ teaspoon salt in a mortar with pestle. When a smooth paste is formed transfer to a mixing bowl. Remove all traces of egg white from yolks using a piece of egg shell. Using a balloon whisk blend egg yolks into garlic, beating well. Gradually add 2 teaspoons lemon juice and beat until light. Gradually add oil, drop by drop at first, beating vigorously. Only add more as each drop is absorbed.

When one-third of oil is added, remainder may be added in a steady trickle, beating constantly. Add remaining lemon juice and if too thick, beat in cold water, a teaspoon at a time. Aioli should hold its shape when whisk is lifted. Adjust seasoning with salt and add pepper to taste. Serve in a bowl or sauceboat.

MAYONNAISE
Proceed as for Aioli, omitting garlic. Begin by beating egg yolks with ¼ teaspoon dry mustard powder, then add lemon juice and oil as above.

Unto

A good Spanish cook always uses a small piece of this pungent pork fat in any dried bean dish. As it is easy enough to prepare at home, I have included directions, particularly for those of Spanish blood living elsewhere who might recollect it, but can't remember how mother made it.

piece of pork flare fat
plain flour
coarse pickling salt

The flare fat is found on the inner rib (loin) section of the pig carcase. It is usually about 10 cm (4 inches) wide, at least twice as long and 6 mm (3/8 inch) thick. Your meat supplier should be able to provide it for you.

Rub flour into the smooth side of the fat with finger tips. Turn fat over and press a thick coating of salt on the other side. Roll up firmly, then tie with white string, securing it over the ends as well to keep the salt in. Hang in a cool place with cheesecloth draped over it for protection and leave for 2-3 weeks until dried. The fat should be slightly pliable. Store in a sealed container in a cool place. Cut off pieces as required, brushing off the salt.

Coconut Milk

1 cup (4 oz) desiccated or grated unsweetened coconut
1¼ cups (10 fl oz) cold water

Place coconut and water in a small pan, stir well and bring slowly to simmering point. Pour into blender jar and blend at high speed for one minute. Place a fine meshed strainer over a bowl and pour in coconut liquid. Press with back of a spoon to extract all liquid. This yields about one cup thick coconut milk. Return coconut from sieve to saucepan. Add more water and repeat procedure. Resultant liquid is thin coconut milk. Store in sealed containers in refrigerator and use as specified in recipes.

Spiced Peanuts and Coconut

Makes about 2 cups

1 cup desiccated coconut
2 tablespoons peanut oil
1 small onion, finely chopped
1 clove garlic, crushed
1 teaspoon grated fresh ginger
1 teaspoon ground coriander
½ teaspoon ground cummin
¼–½ teaspoon chili powder
1 teaspoon salt
1 cup (6 oz) shelled, roasted peanuts

Put coconut in a dry, heated frying pan and stir over low heat until golden. Take care not to burn it. Remove to a bowl.

Heat oil in the pan and add onion. Fry gently until transparent, add ginger and continue frying on higher heat until onion becomes golden brown and crisp. Stir in garlic, coriander, cummin and chili powder. Cook 1 minute longer, then add peanuts and fry, stirring often, for further minute or so. Pour onto coconut, mix well and serve as an accompaniment to Indian meals or as directed in recipes.

Tortillas

The corn tortillas of Mexico require a white corn meal called masa harina not generally available outside Mexico and North America. While corn tortillas are more widely available canned or frozen, wheat tortillas may be substituted if these are unavailable in your area. As these are very similar in preparation to the chapatis of India, follow the Chapati recipe using plain white (all-purpose) flour instead of wholemeal, and lard may be used instead of oil.

Cook on an ungreased griddle or heavy frying pan heated on medium-high heat, and press the tortilla gently all over with a folded cloth to encourage small blisters to form while cooking. Tortillas should cook in about 1½-2 minutes.

To ensure they remain soft as well as warm, have the folded cloth in a large plastic bag, place the tortillas as they are cooked within the cloth and tuck the open end of the bag underneath.

Tortillas may be cooked ahead, cooled in the cloth to keep them soft, then wrapped in foil. Store in freezer.

To heat corn and wheat tortillas: If frozen, thaw in their wrapping in the refrigerator for several hours, or at room temperature. Heat a griddle or heavy frying pan on medium high heat. Put in a tortilla and heat for about 1 minute, turning frequently with tongs. Stack in a folded cloth within a plastic bag. Serve in a folded napkin.

To make taco shells: Though corn tortillas are traditional, wheat tortillas may be used. Put oil in a wide pan to a depth of 1 cm (½ inch). Heat to 180°C (350°F) and fry each tortilla separately, turning with tongs. While tortilla is soft fold in half holding the sides apart with tongs. Turn over and keep frying until crisp. Drain on paper towels. Prepared taco shells are widely available.

Mexican Tomato-Chili Sauce

Makes: about 2½ cups

Not quite like the sauce they make in Mexico as the range of chilis available outside Mexico is not as varied. However this is a good basic sauce to serve with Mexican dishes. The heat can be varied according to taste.

1-2 large green sweet peppers
1 large onion, chopped
2 tablespoons oil
2 cloves garlic, chopped
2-6 dried bird's eye, pequin or tepin chilis
500 g (1 lb) tomatoes, peeled and chopped
½ teaspoon dried oregano
salt to taste

If long, slender, mild peppers are available, use two of these rather than 1 sweet bell pepper. Cut off stem and remove seeds and white membrane. Chop roughly. Place in a pan with onion and oil and cook on medium heat until onion is soft, stirring often. Add garlic and chilis (2 for mild heat, more if you can tolerate hot flavours). Fry for a few seconds then add remaining ingredients, using canned tomatoes for convenience. Cover and simmer for 30 minutes. Pour into blender and blend until smooth. Serve immediately or store in a screw-topped jar in refrigerator and re-heat when required. Serve in place of canned or packaged taco sauce, or as directed in recipes.

Bean Curd

Makes: about 300 g (10 oz)

2½ cups (1 lb) soya beans
cold water
2 tablespoons strained lemon juice or white vinegar

Wash soya beans, place in a bowl and cover with about 3 cups cold water. Leave to soak for 4-6 hours, no longer. Drain and rinse quickly under cold water. Place a quarter of the beans and ½ cup water in food processor fitted with steel blade and process until smooth, scraping down sides occasionally. Turn into a large bowl. Repeat with remaining beans and more water. Add another 4 cups water (with water used in grinding, 3 imperial pints altogether).

Set a colander over a deep bowl and line with a damp, double thickness of butter muslin or cheese cloth (or use a jelly bag). Pour in soya bean liquid and gather ends of cloth. Tie securely and suspend from a fixed object. Remove colander and leave bowl underneath to catch the milk. Leave for 6-8 hours squeezing bag gently now and then to encourage more dripping. Put soya milk in a pan and bring to the boil. Remove from heat, leave 5 minutes and lift skin off carefully placing it on an oiled baking sheet (more about this later). Gently stir in lemon juice or vinegar – curds should begin to form immediately. Cover and leave until cool.

Rinse out the material used for the first dripping process and repeat the process – this time letting the whey drain away. Leave for 8-10 hours. Turn ball of curd carefully onto a flat dish and cut into 2.5cm (1 inch) slices. Place another flat dish on top of the curd and weigh down with weights (use canned goods). Place in refrigerator and leave for 4 hours. Drain off liquid, place bean curd in a container and cover with cold water. Store in refrigerator, changing water daily. Should keep for 1 week.

Taufu kee: Let bean curd skin dry at room temperature for 24 hours, store in a sealed container. Fry in hot oil and add to vegetable dishes, or soak in hot water for 15 minutes and use in same way.

Tahini Cream Sauce

Makes: about 1¾ cups

Tahini is an oily paste made from toasted sesame seeds and available from Armenian, Greek, Middle East and health food stores. While it is now being made locally, the best tahini is usually imported from Greece or the Middle East. The local product is of even, pouring consistency, but imported brands usually separate because of the lapse in time after production. Store unopened tins upside down in your pantry for several days so that the paste may be blended more easily when opened.

2 cloves garlic
salt
¾ cup (6 fl oz) tahini
1 tablespoon white vinegar
juice of 1 lemon
½ cup (4 fl oz) water
½ cup chopped parsley

Crush garlic cloves with ½ teaspoon salt. Place tahini in mixing bowl and beat well. This preliminary beating reduces the strong flavour of the tahini. Beat in garlic and vinegar. Gradually add lemon juice alternately with water. To make a cream sauce of good consistency add enough lemon juice to make the tahini very thick before adding water. This way you have more scope in adjusting the flavour and consistency of the sauce. Add salt to taste, and more lemon juice if a sharper sauce is required. Blend in parsley and chill until required. Serve as directed in recipes.

White Sauce

Makes 2 cups (1 imperial pint)

To be sure of getting the right consistency, use either the cup and spoon measures given, or the weights and liquid measures given in parentheses. If too thick, thin down with a little more milk during end of cooking.

4 tablespoons (2 oz) butter
4 tablespoons (2 oz) flour
2 cups (1 imperial pint) milk
1 teaspoon salt
freshly ground white pepper

Melt butter in a heavy pan and stir in flour. Cook for 2 minutes without allowing flour to colour. Remove from heat and pour in milk all at once, stirring constantly. Return to heat and continue stirring until sauce thickens and bubbles. If sauce becomes lumpy, stir with a balloon whisk. Add salt and pepper to taste and let sauce simmer gently for 3 minutes. If not to be used immediately, press a piece of buttered greaseproof paper over surface of sauce to prevent skin forming. Use as directed in recipes.

Bean Sprouts

Makes: about 2 cups

¼ cup (2 oz) mung beans, adzuki beans or whole brown lentils
water

1 oz. = enough for coffee jar

Wash beans or lentils, place in a bowl and cover with 2 cups cold water. Leave to soak for 8-10 hours. Drain and rinse well. Place in a dark glass jar and secure a single thickness of butter muslin or cheese cloth over the top of the jar with a rubber band. Twice each day, say morning and night, run water into the jar, swirl and pour out, doing this 2 or 3 times. Leave jar upside down for a while on a rack so that liquid can drain out completely. After 4-5 days sprouts should be ready. Keep jar near the kitchen sink so that you will remember to rinse them.

Once sprouted, tip into a deep bowl and fill with water. Swirl gently and scoop off floating skins. Drain well in a colander. When thoroughly drained, put in a sealed container and store in refrigerator. They should keep well for a week. Rinse well before using, and nip off any browned tails.

Note: Frequently imported beans and lentils are fumigated to prevent the spread of plant disease. Because of this practice, such pulses cannot be sprouted. Look for pulses marked as suitable for sprouting.

Arab Flat Bread

PITA

Makes 8 large or 12 smaller breads
Oven temperature: 260°C (500°F)

6 cups (1½ lb) plain (all-purpose) flour
1 sachet (2 teaspoons) active dry yeast
2 cups (1 imperial pint) warm water
1½ teaspoons salt
1 teaspoon sugar
2 tablespoons oil

Sift flour in a large, warm mixing bowl, remove 2 cups flour and set aside. Make a well in the centre of the flour. Dissolve yeast in ¼ cup warm water, add remaining water and stir in salt and sugar. Pour yeast mixture into centre of flour and stir in a little of the flour to thicken liquid. Cover and leave in a warm place until frothy. Beat until smooth by hand for 10 minutes, or on electric mixer with dough hook for 5 minutes.

Sprinkle some of the reserved flour onto a board, turn out dough and knead 10 minutes, using more flour as required. When smooth and satiny, shape into a ball. Oil bowl, put in dough and turn to coat with oil. Stretch plastic film over bowl and leave in a warm place until doubled in bulk – about 45-60 minutes. Preheat oven.

Punch down dough and turn out onto lightly floured board. Knead a little, then divide into 8 or 12 even sized pieces, rolling each into a ball. Roll each piece to a flat round with rolling pin. Place rounds on a floured cloth and cover with another cloth. Rest breads for 20 minutes.

Heat a baking sheet in oven (on lowest shelf in electric oven, top shelf in gas oven). Grease hot baking sheet and quickly and carefully lift 1 or 2 rounds onto sheet. Return to same position in oven and bake for 4-5 minutes until bread puffs up. Turn quickly and return for 1 minute to lightly brown other side. Remove bread and wrap in a cloth to keep it warm and soft. Bake remaining loaves. Store bread in freezer, well wrapped, if not to be eaten for a day of two.

Note 1 sachet active dry yeast may be replaced by 30 g (1 oz) compressed yeast or 1 yeast cake (approximately ½ oz). The latter two are entirely different; compressed yeast is used in Australia and the U.K., while cake yeast is used in North America.

Toasted Avocado Leaves

In Mexican bean cooking, there are three additives used interchangeably, each claimed as preventing the discomfort beans can cause. Besides their medicinal qualities, fresh coriander (Chinese parsley), dried oregano and toasted, dried avocado leaves add their own particular flavour to the bean dish. While the first two are well-known as herbs, avocado leaf as an additive is little known outside Mexico, and is well-worth trying. Of course, you need access to an avocado tree.

To grow a tree all you require is an avocado seed. Insert 3 cocktail picks or match sticks about 2.5 cm (1 inch) above the end of the seed with the slight hollow or flaw, or the pointed end depending on the species of avocado. Fill a jar with water and put seed on top, with the sticks supporting the seed on the rim to allow air space. The base of the seed must be immersed in the water, so top up as required. Leave in a light place until roots form and shoot appears, then plant in a large pot or in the garden. In 6-8 months you should have a sturdy plant to provide leaves. If it bears fruit in seven years count yourself very fortunate indeed.

To dry leaves: Cut sprigs of leaves from plant, tie in a bunch and hang in an airy place until dry. Dried leaves are available in Mexican markets in the United States.

To toast leaves: Put required number of dried leaves on a heated griddle or under heated grill (broiler) and toast, turning often, until lightly browned and crisp. Use whole toasted leaves to top bean casseroles when cooking (they do not have to be Mexican in origin), or crumble toasted leaves to a fine powder and sprinkle on top of cooked bean dishes. The whole leaves are removed after the casserole is cooked; crumbled leaves are blended into the cooked beans.

Bean Curd Dressing

Makes: about 1 cup

⅓ cup (3 fl oz) salad oil
¼ cup (2 fl oz) cider vinegar
2 pieces bean curd, each about 5 cm (2 inches) square
½ teaspoon chopped fresh ginger
1 small clove garlic, optional
2 drops tabasco sauce
salt

Put ingredients in blender jar, adding salt to taste. Blend until smooth, adjust seasoning and use immediately. Dressing may be chilled until required. Depending on type of oil used, dressing may have to be brought to room temperature and beaten just before use as some oils congeal when chilled. Use the dressing on tossed green salads, bean and bean sprout salads.

. . . AND SOMETHING SWEET

Most of us have a sweet tooth, but how does one justify such a section in a bean cookbook? Simple! Peanuts, carob and tamarind are all members of the family – the peanuts and carob in particular lend themselves admirably to sweet delights. You will also find sweets and puddings which actually use beans from countries which have thoroughly explored the versatility of the bean.

Peanut Brittle

Makes: about 600 g (1¼ lb) brittle

2 cups (1 lb) granulated sugar
½ cup (4 fl oz) water
2 tablespoons liquid glucose or light corn syrup
1 cup (6 oz) roasted peanuts, skins rubbed off and split
3 teaspoons butter
pinch salt
1 teaspoon bicarbonate of soda

Put sugar, water and glucose or corn syrup into a deep, heavy pan and place on medium heat. Stir now and again with a wooden spoon to dissolve sugar as crystals must dissolve before mixture boils. When dissolved wipe down sides of pan with a bristle brush dipped in cold water to remove any sugar crystals. Remove spoon and let toffee boil on same heat for about 20-25 minutes until golden (150°C or 300°F on candy thermometer). While toffee is cooking have peanuts ready, butter measured and set aside, and salt mixed in with soda, breaking up any lumps. Grease a large marble slab or stainless steel tray with butter.

When toffee is ready remove from heat, add peanuts, butter and soda mixture and stir in lightly until toffee foams. Pour onto slab or tray and leave a few minutes until cool enough to handle. Pull out gently until very thin. Wear a pair of clean rubber gloves to protect fingers as toffee must be pulled before edges begin to set. When cold, break into pieces and store in an airtight container.

Peanut Butter Bread

Oven Temperature: 190-200°C (375-400°F)

1 cup (4 oz) plain (all-purpose) flour
1 cup (4 oz) wholemeal flour
4 teaspoons baking powder
¾ cup (6 oz) brown sugar
1 cup (4oz) smooth peanut butter
¼ cup (2 oz) butter
1 egg
¾ cup (6 fl oz) milk
Nut topping:
1 tablespoon butter
1 tablespoon honey
1 tablespoon brown sugar
¼ cup (1 oz) chopped roasted peanuts

Sift flours and baking powder into a mixing bowl, adding any bran to bowl which doesn't pass through sifter. Add brown sugar and blend in with fingers to break up sugar lumps. Blend peanut butter with butter, cut into flour with a knife, then rub in lightly with fingertips. Beat egg lightly and combine with milk. Pour into flour mixture and mix until thoroughly combined without over-mixing. Turn into a greased and floured 20 x 10 cm (8 x 4 inch) loaf tin and bake in a moderately hot oven for 45 minutes. Spread topping on loaf and cook for further 15 minutes. Invert onto a wire rack covered with foil, turn right side up on rack to cool. Replace any topping from foil onto loaf if necessary. Serve sliced, spread with cream cheese or butter and honey.

Nut topping: Blend ingredients in a saucepan and heat just long enough to combine.

Peanut Butter French Toast

Makes 8 slices

¼ cup smooth peanut butter
¾ cup (6 fl oz) milk
2 eggs
8 thick slices white bread
¼ cup (2 oz) butter

Put peanut butter in a shallow dish and gradually blend in milk. Lightly beat eggs and stir into milk mixture.

Heat 1 tablespoon butter in a frying pan until foaming. Dip 2 slices bread into mixture, transfer to pan and cook until golden brown on each side. Repeat with remaining bread, adding more butter to pan as required. Serve with jam, jelly preserves, honey or maple syrup. An excellent breakfast treat or a snack at any time.

Peanut Cream Pie

Oven Temperature: 200°C (400°F) reducing to 180°C (350°F)

Pie Crust:
1 cup (4 oz) plain (all-purpose) flour
¼ teaspoon salt
⅓ cup (3 oz) butter or margarine
1 egg, separated
cold water
Peanut Filling:
2 eggs, separated
¾ cup (6 oz) brown sugar
¼ cup (2 oz) crunchy peanut butter
½ teaspoon vanilla essence
½ cup (4 fl oz) milk
To finish:
½ cup (4 fl oz) thick cream, whipped
1 tablespoon caster (fine) sugar
¼ teaspoon vanilla essence
½ cup chopped roasted peanuts

Sift flour and salt into mixing bowl and cut in shortening until mixture resembles fine crumbs. Combine egg yolk with 2 teaspoons water and blend in, adding a little more water if necessary to hold pastry together. Knead lightly, cover and rest in a cool place for 15 minutes. Roll out and line a 23 cm (9 inch) pie plate. Trim and crimp edge. Do not prick base. Beat egg white lightly and brush about 1 teaspoon of this over base and sides of pastry. Leave aside to rest and dry a little. Beat egg yolks with brown sugar using a wooden spoon, breaking up any sugar lumps. Blend in peanut butter and vanilla and stir in milk.

Add remaining egg white from pastry to the two egg whites and beat until stiff. Fold into peanut butter mixture and pour into pie crust. Bake in a pre-heated hot oven for 20 minutes, reduce to moderate and bake for further 20 minutes or until cooked when tested as you would a custard. Cool completely.

Fold caster sugar and vanilla into whipped cream and spread in rough peaks on pie. Sprinkle with chopped peanuts just before serving.

Mung Bean and Coconut Dessert

Serves: 6-8

In Sri Lanka this is called mung ata, a popular sweetmeat which traditionally uses jaggery (palm sugar). If you can get this ingredient use it in place of the brown sugar given in the recipe. Fresh coconut must be used; remove brown skin from flesh and grate flesh on a hand grater or break into pieces and process in food processor using steel blade.

1 cup (8 oz) mung beans
4 cups (2 imperial pints) water
¼ teaspoon salt
1 cup (5 oz) grated fresh coconut
½ cup (4 oz) brown sugar
For serving:
additional grated fresh coconut
1 cup thick coconut milk (page 105)

Pick over mung beans and wash well. Place in a pan with water and bring to the boil. Reduce heat, cover and boil gently without stirring for 1 hour or until beans are very soft. Remove lid and let any moisture evaporate. Stir in coconut and brown sugar and serve hot or warm in little pudding bowls. Additional coconut and coconut milk should be added according to individual taste.

Sweet Red Bean Paste

Makes: about 2 cups

1 cup (8 oz) adzuki beans
3 cups (1½ imperial pints) water
¾ cup (6 oz) granulated sugar
½ cup peanut oil
1-2 teaspoons rose water

Pick over beans and wash well. Put in a pan with the water and soak for 2 hours. Bring to the boil, cover and boil gently for 2-2½ hours until very soft and most of the liquid is absorbed. If beans dry out before they are cooked, add more water. Alternatively cook beans in pressure cooker for 20 minutes. (See page 10 .)

Purée beans and remaining liquid in food processor or blender, or press through a sieve. Return to a heavy pan with sugar and peanut oil. Cook on medium low heat for 25-30 minutes until paste just holds its shape when stirred. Stir occasionally while cooking and take care that paste does not scorch. Blend in rose water to taste and cool. Store in a screw-top jar in refrigerator and use as directed in recipes.

Tamarind Syrup

500 g (1 lb) tamarind pods
4 cups (2 imperial pints) hot water
4 cups (2 lb) granulated sugar

Put pods in a bowl and cover with the hot water. Break up pods in water with fingers, stir then strain off water into another bowl. Let the liquid settle and pour back into bowl containing tamarind, leaving any sediment in the second bowl. This will contain dust particles and should be discarded. Let tamarind soak for 15 to 20 minutes and pass through a fine sieve set over a pan. Rub with the back of a spoon to separate pulp from seeds and fibres. Pour a little more water over tarmarind in sieve to extract all pulp. Discard seeds and fibres. Add sugar to pan and stir over medium heat until sugar is dissolved. Bring to the boil — do not stir once syrup is boiling. Boil on medium heat for 15 minutes or until a little syrup thickens when left on a cold saucer for a few minutes. Remove pan from heat when testing thickness. Return to heat if syrup is too thin — it should be the consistency of thin honey when cool. It is advisable to skim syrup frequently while boiling — this rids the syrup of any remaining impurities. When ready, cool and pour into sterilized bottles. Seal and store in a cool place. To serve dilute syrup with iced water to your taste.

Carob Mousse

Serves: 6

100 g (3½ oz) dark block carob
2 teaspoons unflavoured gelatine
2 tablespoons hot water
2 teaspoons instant coffee powder
3 eggs, separated
¼ cup (2 oz) raw sugar
pinch salt
3 teaspoons rum
½ cup (4 fl oz) whipped cream
For serving:
whipped cream
grated dark block carob

Break up carob into pieces and melt in a bowl set in a hot water bath. Dissolve gelatine in the 2 tablespoons hot water and blend in coffee powder. Stir into melted carob. Put egg yolks and sugar in a heatproof bowl and set over a pan of simmering water. Whisk until light and creamy. Blend in carob mixture, salt and rum. Remove from heat and cool.

Beat egg whites until stiff and fold into carob mixture with whipped cream. Pour into 6 small pots or sweet glasses and chill for 6 hours or longer. Just before serving pipe a swirl of whipped cream on top of each mousse and sprinkle with grated carob.

Carob Peanut Cookies

Makes: 4 dozen cookies or 2 dozen sandwiched cookies
Oven Temperature: 180-190°C (350-375°F)

½ cup (4 oz) butter
½ cup (4 oz) caster (fine) sugar
1 teaspoon vanilla essence
1½ cups (6 oz) plain flour
¼ cup (1 oz) carob powder
1 teaspoon baking powder
¼ cup (2 fl oz) milk
½ cup (2 oz) chopped salted peanuts
Carob Frosting (page 118), optional

Cream butter, sugar and vanilla essence until light and fluffy. Sift dry ingredients and fold into creamed mixture alternately with milk. Blend in chopped peanuts and drop in generous teaspoonfuls on greased baking sheets, keeping the rough mounds as round as possible. Bake in a moderate oven for 20-25 minutes. Cool on baking sheets for 10 minutes, then remove to a wire rack to complete cooling. Serve as they are or sandwich pairs together with Carob Frosting.

Steamed Sweet Bean Buns

Makes: 12 buns

A popular Chinese between-meal snack, nourishing and satisfying. While a yeast dough is traditionally used, one using baking powder is much simpler to make and tastes just as good. Chinese bamboo steamers are readily available – you will need two 25 cm (10 inch) or 3 smaller steamers and a bamboo lid to fit.

Dough:
3 cups (12 oz) plain flour
4 teaspoons baking powder
½ teaspoon salt
¼ cup (2 oz) caster (fine) sugar
¼ cup (2 oz) lard
¾ cup (6 fl oz) warm water
1 teaspoon white vinegar
To finish:
1 230 g (8 oz) can or 1 cup sweet red bean paste (page 114)
sesame oil
greaseproof or waxed paper

Sift flour with baking powder twice. Put into a mixing bowl with sugar and salt. Blend and rub in lard with fingertips until evenly distributed. Combine water with vinegar and pour into flour. Mix to a firm dough, then knead lightly until smooth.

Cover bowl with plastic food wrap and rest dough for 20 minutes. On a lightly floured board roll dough into a long roll and slice into 12 even portions. Roll out or press each portion into a 10 cm (4 inch) round with centre slightly thicker than edges. Put a tablespoon of bean paste in the centre and bring up sides of dough over filling, gathering edges together and pressing well to seal. Twist top to ensure a good seal.

Cut greaseproof or waxed paper into twelve 12 cm (5 inch) squares and brush each piece lightly on one side with sesame oil. Place buns join side down on oiled paper and arrange in bamboo steamers, stacking them and covering top with lid. Have a saucepan or wok filled to one-third with gently boiling water and place steamer over water. If using a pan, diameter must be slightly smaller than base of steamer. Steam for 25 minutes – there is no need to reposition steamers.

Serve hot or warm – these are at their best when freshly cooked though they reheat well in a microwave oven.

Note: A Western-style metal steamer may be used. Place 2 paper towels on top of buns to protect them from condensation. Cook the buns in 2 lots if necessary.

Date and Bean Paste Cakes

Makes: about 30 pieces

A popular sweetmeat in China, and only occasionally served in Chinese restaurants in Western cities. Traditionally the Chinese red date is used, but pitted cooking dates are a very convenient substitute.

250 g (8 oz) pitted dates, chopped
½ cup water
90 g (3 oz) lard
½ cup (5 oz) sweet red bean paste (page 114)
½ cup (4 oz) granulated sugar
1 cup (6 oz) ground rice

Put dates in a heavy pan with water, cover and cook until soft. Remove lid and stir dates over heat to a smooth paste. Blend in lard, bean paste and sugar. Remove pan from heat and stir in ground rice.

Grease a 20 cm (8 inch) square heat proof casserole dish or cake pan with butter. Check that the dish will fit into the utensil used for steaming. Spread paste evenly in dish and cover rim with 2 paper towels. Pull lid on or cover securely with aluminium foil.

Place a rack in a wok and add water to come just below rack. Cover with lid and bring to the boil. Put dish or pan on rack, cover wok and steam for 1 hour. Alternatively dish can be placed in a large bamboo steamer, covered with bamboo lid instead of paper towels and foil, and set over a large pan of boiling water or in a covered wok. When using a bamboo steamer over an ordinary pan, choose a pan slightly smaller in diameter than the steamer.

When cake is cooked, uncover and cool in dish. Chill until firm and cut into small diamond-shaped pieces or squares for serving. Store remainder in refrigerator.

Red Bean Jelly

YOKAN

In Japan this jelly is served as a candy and uses agar agar as the setting agent. Made from seaweed, agar agar is the Asian version of gelatine. Its advantage lies in the fact that it sets without refrigeration. Because it is vegetable in origin, health food stores stock it; also available at Chinese and Japanese food stores. Usually sold in powdered form or strands — I prefer the powdered agar agar as it is easier to gauge quantities.

1 cup (8 oz) adzuki beans
4 cups (2 imperial pints) water
1 cup (8 oz) granulated sugar
additional 3 cups (1½ imperial pints) water
6 teaspoons powdered agar agar

Wash beans well, put in a pan and add the 4 cups water. Soak for 2 hours and bring to the boil. Boil gently, covered, for 2½-3 hours until very soft. Most of water should be absorbed. Rub beans and liquid through a fine sieve set over a bowl. Return to pan and add sugar and additional 2 cups water. Bring to the boil and boil on low heat for 15 minutes.

Blend agar agar into remaining water and add to bean liquid. Return to the boil, stirring occasionally, then pour into two 20 cm (8 inch) square layer cake pans. Leave at room temperature until set. Cut into small squares or diamonds to serve. Jelly should be stored in refrigerator if not to be used immediately.

Carob Layer Cake

Oven Temperature: 180-190°C (350-375°F)

½ cup (2 oz) carob powder
1½ tablespoons (30 g or 1 oz) butter
½ cup (4 fl oz) boiling water
4 eggs
¾ cup (6 oz) caster (fine) sugar
1 teaspoon vanilla essence
1¼ cups (5 oz) plain flour
½ teaspoon bicarbonate of soda
1 teaspoon cream of tartar
pinch salt
whipped, sweetened cream for filling
Carob Frosting:
1 cup (6 oz) icing (confectioner's) sugar
3 teaspoons carob powder
½ teaspoon instant coffee powder
½ teaspoon vanilla essence
1½ tablespoons (30 g or 1 oz) soft butter
1-2 tablespoons milk

Grease two 20 cm (8 inch) layer cake pans with butter and chill. Dust with flour, shaking out excess.

Sift carob powder into a bowl, add butter and pour a little of the boiling water over the butter to soften it. Blend into the carob powder, gradually adding remaining water. Mix until smooth and leave aside to cool.

Beat eggs and sugar until light and foamy and blend in vanilla essence. Sift dry ingredients twice and fold into beaten eggs alternately with carob liquid. Pour into prepared cake pans and bake in a pre-heated moderate oven for 30 minutes or until cooked when tested. Cakes will shrink from sides of pans. Leave in pans for 2 minutes then turn onto wire racks to cool. When cold join layers with whipped, sweetened cream and frost top with Carob Frosting.

To make *Carob Frosting:* Sift icing sugar, carob powder and instant coffee into mixing bowl. Add vanilla essence and blend in soft butter with enough milk to give a good spreading consistency. Beat for a minute or two and swirl on top of cake.

Peanut Muffins

Makes 12–15, depending on size
Oven temperature: 200°C (400°F)

1½ cups (6 oz) plain (all-purpose) flour
3 teaspoons baking powder
¼ teaspoon salt
¼ cup (2 oz) caster (fine) sugar
½ cup (2 oz) finely chopped roasted peanuts
1 egg, beaten
⅔ cup (6 fl oz) milk
¼ cup (2 oz) melted butter
additional 2 tablespoons chopped peanuts

Sift flour, baking powder and salt twice and place in mixing bowl. Blend in sugar and the ½ cup peanuts and make a well in the centre. Pour egg, milk and cool melted butter into well and stir in dry ingredients. Mix lightly and just long enough to blend ingredients; do not over-mix. Batter should be fairly stiff and a little lumpy. Put into greased muffin pans with each pan two-thirds full. Sprinkle tops with the additional chopped peanuts. Bake in a hot oven for 20–25 minutes, depending on size. Serve warm with butter.

Clockwise — Carob Layer Cake, above; Carob Peanut Cookies, page 115; Peanut Brittle, page 111; Carob Mousse, page 115; and Mexican Spiced Peanuts, page 38.

Tamarind and Cummin Drink

This Indian beverage is often taken with meals as a digestive. Normally it is made with the tamarind, ginger, spices and a little sugar. I have used the Tamarind Syrup recipe as a basis which upsets the balance, but is quicker to prepare once you have the syrup on hand. Either add ¼ cup tamarind water to the quantity given below, or add lemon juice as suggested.

½ cup Tamarind Syrup (page 114)
3 teaspoons grated fresh ginger
2 teaspoons ground cummin
pinch chili powder, optional
½ teaspoon garam masala
pinch salt
1½ cups cold water
1 tablespoon lemon juice
For serving:
ice cubes
mint sprigs
lemon slices

Combine tamarind syrup with ginger, cummin, chili powder if used, garam masala, salt and water. Add lemon juice or the tamarind water mentioned in introduction to recipe. Stir well and strain through a muslin-lined sieve. Quarter-fill a glass with this liquid and add ice cubes and water to fill glass. Garnish with mint and lemon. Serve with meals or as a refreshing drink.

Carob Ice Cream

Makes about 2 litres (3½ imperial pints or 4½ US pints)

2 teaspoons unflavoured gelatin
¼ cup (2 fl oz) water
¼ cup (1 oz) carob powder
1 tablespoon butter
1½ cups (12 fl oz) evaporated milk, chilled
⅔ cup (5 oz) caster (fine) sugar
1 teaspoon vanilla essence
pinch salt

Soften gelatin in water in a small pan. Heat gently until dissolved. Add sifted carob powder and butter and stir until butter melts. Cool thoroughly.

Put well-chilled milk in a large bowl and whip until tripled in volume. Beat in sugar, vanilla essence, salt and cooled carob mixture. Pour into deep refrigerator trays or a plastic ice cream container, cover and freeze until set around the edges. Turn into a chilled bowl and beat until creamy — about 1 minute on electric mixer. Return to container, cover and freeze.

Raisin-Rum: Soak ½ cup (3 oz) chopped, seedless raisins in 2 tablespoons dark rum for 2 hours in refrigerator. Fold into ice cream after second beating.

Peanut Brittle: Fold ¾ cup coarsely crushed peanut brittle into ice cream after second beating.

Cassoulet, page 49.

Carob Fudge

Makes about 60 pieces

3 cups (1½ lb) granulated sugar
¼ cup (1oz) carob powder
1 cup (½ imperial pint) milk
¼ cup (2 oz) butter
3 teaspoons honey
1 teaspoon vanilla essence
1 cup (6 oz) shelled, roasted peanuts, optional

Put sugar, sifted carob powder and milk in a heavy pan and heat, stirring occasionally, until sugar is dissolved. Add butter and honey and bring to the boil. Insert a candy thermometer at this stage if you have one (heat it first in hot water). Boil steadily on medium heat for 30–35 minutes, until thermometer reaches 115°C (240°F) or when a few drops of fudge in cold water can be gathered into a soft ball. Remove from heat and leave 5 minutes.

Stir in vanilla essence and peanuts if used, then beat with a wooden spoon until thickened and creamy. Do not beat past this stage as fudge will not spread. If this happens, stir in a little cream. Spread into a greased 18 x 28 cm (7 x 11 inch) slab cake pan. Cut while warm into 2 cm (¾ inch) squares with a sharp knife. Cool and store pieces in an airtight container.

Peanut Crisps

Makes about 60
Oven temperature: 180°C (350°F)

2 cups shelled, roasted peanuts
1¼ cups (5 oz) plain flour
¼ teaspoon salt
¾ cup granulated sugar
½ cup (4 oz) butter
2 tablespoons golden or dark corn syrup
1 teaspoon bicarbonate of soda
2 tablespoons boiling water

Rub husks off peanuts if present. Grind half the peanuts coarsely in food processor (or use 1 cup ready ground peanuts). Split remaining peanuts into halves. Place ground and halved peanuts into a bowl and add flour sifted with salt, and the sugar. Mix well to combine. Melt butter in a pan with the syrup. Blend soda into boiling water and pour into heated butter. Stir well and when frothy pour into bowl. Mix thoroughly with a wooden spoon. Shape heaped teaspoons of mixture in balls and place on lightly greased baking sheets, spacing them well apart to allow for spreading. Bake in a moderate oven for 15 minutes or until golden brown. Leave on sheets for 2 minutes and lift off with a wide spatula to wire rack to cool. They will become crisp on cooling. Store in an airtight container.

Carob Chiffon Pie

Oven temperature: 210°C (425°F)

Peanut Pie Crust:
1 cup (4 oz) plain (all-purpose) flour
½ teaspoon baking powder
½ teaspoon salt
1 tablespoon caster (fine) sugar
⅓ cup (2½ oz) butter
¼ cup (1 oz) finely chopped roasted peanuts
cold water
Carob Chiffon Filling:
3 teaspoons unflavoured gelatin
¼ cup (2 fl oz) water
¼ cup (1 oz) carob powder
¾ cup (6 oz) caster (fine) sugar
¼ teaspoon salt
¼ teaspoon cinnamon
¾ cup (6 fl oz) milk
3 eggs, separated
1 teaspoon Vanilla essence
1tablespoon dark rum
½ cup (4 fl oz) whipping cream
To finish:
whipped cream
1 tablespoon finely chopped peanuts

Sift flour, baking powder, salt and sugar into a bowl and rub in butter until mixture resembles fine crumbs. Blend in peanuts and mix in enough cold water (2-3 tablespoons) until dough holds together. Pastry can be prepared in food processor. Knead lightly, roll in plastic film and rest 10 minutes. Roll out on a floured board to a 28 cm (11 inch) circle and line an ungreased 23 cm (9 inch) pie pan. Fold edge under to build up rim. Crimp edge, prick base and sides with a fork and bake in a hot oven for 12-15 minutes until cooked. Leave to cool thoroughly.

Sprinkle gelatin into water in a small bowl and leave to soak. Blend sifted carob powder, ½ cup of the sugar, salt and cinnamon in a heavy pan and stir in milk. Place on medium heat and bring to the boil. Stir in soaked gelatin and remove from heat. (Do not be concerned if mixture looks as though it has curdled.) Beat egg yolks in a bowl and blend in a little of the hot carob mixture. Pour egg yolks into pan and stir over heat for 2 minutes. Remove, pour into a bowl and stir in vanilla essence and rum. Chill, stirring occasionally, until thickened but not set.

Whip cream. Beat egg whites until soft peaks form and gradually beat in remaining sugar. Beat until glossy. Fold whipped cream into egg whites, then fold this mixture into the thickened carob custard. Use a metal spoon to blend mixtures thoroughly and quickly. Pour into cooled crust and chill until set. Before serving top with whipped cream and sprinkle with peanuts.

Note: The filling makes an excellent dessert without the crust.

Carob Coated Dates

Makes 20

20 dessert dates
¼ cup (1½ oz) roasted, shelled peanuts
75 g (2½ oz) dark block carob
¼ teaspoon ground cinnamon, optional

Pit the dates if necessary. Rub husks from shelled peanuts if necessary. Insert one or two peanuts into dates and press dates to enclose peanuts.

Break carob into pieces and put into a heat-proof bowl. Place bowl in a pan of water and heat water. When carob begins to melt in base of bowl, remove pan from heat and let carob melt slowly, stirring now and then. Too much heat will make finished confections dull.

When carob is melted, stir in cinnamon if used. Dip dates into carob to coat, using two fine skewers to turn dates and lift them out onto waxed paper. Leave until firm and store in an airtight container in a cool place (not the refrigerator). Serve with after-dinner coffee.

WEIGHTS AND MEASURES

Cooking should be a relaxing occupation without the need to fiddle with scales and exact liquid measures. However, I concede that some cooks have been conditioned to accurate weights and measures. Personally I prefer using standard cup and spoon measures, and because Australia, the United States, Canada and United Kingdom beg to differ, I have taken the standard measures of these countries into consideration in testing the recipes.

Therefore when working with cup measures, use either the 250ml cup (Australia and New Zealand), the 300ml cup (U.K.), or the 8 fl oz cup (U.S. and Canada), and retain these cup measures throughout the recipe.

If you prefer to weigh ingredients then follow the amounts given in parentheses which, in relation to dried beans, is a little greater than all but a 300ml cup measure.

The liquid measures in parentheses are in proportion to the weight of the dried pulses etc.

For measures up to 1 cup I have taken 8 fluid ounces as the cup measure and though this is not consistent with the imperial pint measure the difference is minimal, will not affect recipes and has been chosen for convenience.

Had I taken a half imperial pint (10 fl oz) as a cup measure, it makes fractional cups a little awkward to translate into fluid measures.

The other area of difference between the countries is in the tablespoon measure.

While the Australian tablespoon has a liquid capacity of 20mls, the U.K. tablespoon is 15mls in capacity and the U.S. tablespoon is ½ fluid ounce (near enough to 15mls).

Where tablespoon measurements are crucial these have been given in teaspoons as on this point we all agree. Otherwise use your standard tablespoon measure.

Meats, poultry, fish and vegetables have been given in both metric and imperial (or avoirdupois) weights for the purposes of marketing, though a few grams or ounces one way or another will not affect the success of your dish.

SWITCHING BEANS

While recipes specify certain beans, more often than not other beans would work just as well. In fact some substitute beans will give a new flavour and texture to traditional bean recipes, making your range of bean dishes even greater.

Bean and lentil varieties only are listed, with the recipes using that particular pulse and other recipes which can be adapted to it. Bean curd, bean sprout and peanut recipes are listed in the general Index.

If you are just beginning to do more bean cooking, the groupings under specific beans will show you at a glance just what variety of dishes a certain bean or lentil will give you, and you can market accordingly. Knowing which other beans can be substituted can also be a great advantage when certain beans are unavailable in your area.

When using any of the recipes listed, and the actual recipe does not give details of the bean you intend using, then check cooking times given for specific beans, pages 14 to 17. However soya beans are the only ones which will require special care and longer cooking; as Egyptian brown beans are unfamiliar to many, I have given directions for adaptation after the recipe names.

INDEX